RADICAL UNSCHOOLING

A Revolution Has Begun

BY

Dayna Martin

Radical Unschooling
A Revolution Has Begun

Dayna Martin
196 East Madison Road
Madison, NH 03849
USA

Website:
www.Dayna-Martin.com

Cover Photo, left to right:
Devin, Ivy, Joe, Orion, Dayna and Dakota Martin

Cover and back photos by Jessica Niles www.capturedbyjess.wordpress.com

Cover and Book Design by Dayna Martin

Dedication

This book was written for children everywhere in the hopes that they will be seen as the whole people I know they are.

Children are living now, not tomorrow. When we, as a culture, can move from trying to control children to trying to connect with them, everything will shift, consciousness will raise and parenting as we know it will evolve.

Acknowledgements

I want to thank my husband, Joe, truly my other half,
for his patience, his beautiful open mind and his loving, kind heart.

Thank you to my friend and mentor, Barb Lundgren for her wisdom and inspiration.

I also want to thank my mother, Darlene -
my best friend and biggest supporter in all that I do or dream about.

Finally, I want to thank my sweet children, for if it weren't for them,
I wouldn't be the whole person that I am today.

I love you Devin, Dakota, Ivy and Orion.
Thank you for your unconditional love, laughter and beauty.

The World needs you.

Table of Contents

Welcome to Radical Unschooling

by

Dr. Caron B. Goode

How much heartache we would save ourselves if we would recognize children as partners with adults in the process of living, rather than always viewing them as apprentices. How much we could teach each other; we have the experience and they have the freshness. How full both our lives could be.

John A. Taylor

In this far-reaching book, Dayna Martin introduces the concept of radical unschooling as a parenting philosophy about how to facilitate her children's living and learning. Her children chase their individual passions while she pursues hers by offering this newest guide to a growing grass-roots movement called Radical Unschooling.

As a noun, the word *radical* is a person who advocates through reform. As an adjective, the word *radical* means sweeping and far-reaching—the kind of influence Dayna will forge in the coming decades.

So the movement called radical unschooling has begun, and its advocate is Dayna

Martin, an inspirational speaker, assertive author and loving friend, wife and parent. You will not find a more passionate person representing radical unschooling philosophy.

The principles of radical unschooling include being responsive to children in the moment, and yet responding authentically. Dayna gives parents permission to dump the guilt and follow their instinct and heart in parenting with purpose, passion and awareness. The results are children whose natural curiosity guides their learning. In the radical unschooling parenting model, children do not follow curricula, are not compared to others or put down or praised falsely through report cards. Children are not forced into unnatural social situations or forced to live someone else's agenda or ideas for performance.

At its basics, *Radical Unschooling* opens your mind to parenting and to facilitating children's learning through heart, optimism and awareness.

In the following pages, you'll find a positive approach to facilitating children's learning through their interests and passions. Unschooling does not look like the average picture of homeschooling, such as a mom and her kids gathered around the kitchen table doing workbook pages while following a curriculum.

Unschooling looks like what you would picture a child doing on a weekend or vacation, such as joyfully building a fort in the woods, enjoying a game with their parents, or taking a day trip somewhere special. The focus is on happiness and a loving connection with one another. It also involves seeing the learning in all that your children do.

If you are seeking new ideas, natural parenting, parenting with heart and intuition or being authentic, then open the pages to find true and delightful stories of how radical unschooling works. At the end, you'll have a more open mind for your child's rights and choices, as well as a new perspective on what is possible in this leading-edge approach to parenting.

Dr. Caron Goode,

Author, *Raising Intuitive Children* (New Page Press, 2009)

Introduction

My name is **Dayna Martin**, partner to Joe and mother to four children, who have never been to school. I am a **Radical Unschooling advocate**. On any given day, no matter where I am, I am connecting with my children as they explore their own passions. Their passions become mine as I bring more and more of their interests into their lives. **I know that whatever they are exploring at the time is the nucleus of their learning, and their interests expand into wondrous directions.**

Whether Dakota and I try out a new recipe in the kitchen, or I explore a new computer game with my son Devin, my role is to be involved and to learn about their interests along side of them. There is no other time that I feel more connected with my children than when we are doing something that they love. I know that learning never has to be forced. Learning feels good, and this *joy* of life and learning is the basis of our lives and radical unschooling philosophy.

My second passion in life is helping those who want to become advocates for unschooling find their unique form of advocacy. What brought me to unschooling was a progression of learning to listen to my instincts as a woman and mother. I became an advocate for the rights and respect of children after I birthed my first child. This started the path of attachment parenting for me as I tuned into and valued the needs of my son. **Attachment parenting is a natural, instinctual approach to parenting where emotional bonds of parent and child are nurtured.**

12

After giving birth to Devin, my first child, I wore him in a sling all day, slept with him by my side and fed him as often as he wanted. This felt so right, so perfect to me. I was so in tune with my child that parenting was a pleasurable experience. This was such a contrast to what I saw my friends going through. I knew that I had discovered a parenting secret that others needed to know about.

By the time my second child Dakota was born, I had become a Natural Childbirth Educator, breastfeeding counselor and Doula. As I helped others on the path of natural childbirth and attachment parenting, I felt empowered, like I was fulfilling a destiny. My personal advocacy grew as I had more children. I wrote for well-known magazines and befriended other advocates who inspired me. The more people I reached, the more my passion grew.

Radical unschooling is a natural extension of attachment parenting and the movement is helping to shift human consciousness. When we embrace the respect that children deserve as we raise them, we change the meaning of parenting today. **Parenting is supposed to be joyful, and it can be when we learn how to connect with, rather than control our children.**

We were raised in a different era where the majority of the parenting focused on *obedience* and doing what we were told. Even the nanny television shows and most programs having to do with parenting today are focused solely on obedience as a main parenting objective. We are used to being told what to do in our culture from our parents, and also from the overall lessons learned in school. We are trained to believe that life is about taking orders, however subtle those orders may seem. It does take effort and a desire to break free from the *yes-man* type of thinking most of us were raised with. Once you understand that there is a more respectful, fulfilling way to live in harmony with not only our children, but also with others, you are well on your way. **Just learning that a new parenting paradigm exists is often the first step in someone's journey to a new awakening.**

Unschooling, especially radical unschooling, is on the **leading edge of new thought.** Some mornings, I think about how phenomenal the changes will be for our grandchildren. We are the pioneers for this life by living and sharing our truths. We are changing the course of human history by living our lives in freedom, peace and respect with one another. The Revolution Has Begun.

Chapter One

Unschooling Is....

The more intensely we feel about an idea or a goal, the more assuredly the idea, buried deep in our subconscious, will direct us along the path to its fulfillment.

Earl Nightingale

John Holt (1923-1985), an influential educator and visionary, first coined the term, *unschooling*. He was the father of the 1970's unschooling movement, which is an offshoot of homeschooling. Holt was against formal education, most especially forcing children to learn against their will. He believed that a basic right of all humans is the right to choose what they learn and think.

Picking up where Holt left off, I am a strong advocate in our world today. My family and I live a philosophy called *radical unschooling*, based on the belief that children learn best when they are internally motivated. **I see my role not as my child's teacher, but as their life and learning facilitator.** Like Holt, I do not believe a formal education in today's schools is necessary, even optional, for a child's true happiness. In my eyes, happiness is the key to success.

Radical unschooling is passion-driven learning because not everyone is meant to do the same thing in life or to follow one road.

Unschooling includes trusting your child in what they choose to learn. Radical unschooling, which expands unschooling philosophy to parenting, means you extend that same trust to other areas of your child's life, like foods, media, television, video games—allowing them to play or watch whatever they want when they want.

I know this sounds crazy the first time you read it. Extending that same trust to other areas of your child's life, like learning to use the toilet, or television watching, requires thinking outside the box and a huge dose of courage.

Once this philosophy becomes your truth, it gets much easier. Once you see your child's happiness and the learning that takes place as a side effect of living a rich, full life together, your mind expands. You become confident and committed.

Unschooling Moment

There are differing labels for "unschooling," and just as many opinions about the term. Some love it and compare the word to "uncoiling" or "undo-ing." Some folks don't like the fact that it focuses on what we *don't* do as oppose to what we actually *do*.

I've heard labels such as Life Learning, or Organic Learning, or Delight-driven Learning.

In unschooling, we've considered ourselves all of these things at one time of another. Sometimes we are "delight-driven" by exploring a topic that brings us joy. Sometimes we are "surprise-learners" because we had no idea that amazing learning has taken place within us until a later time. I consider myself an "impetuous learner" in the way that I passionately dive into inspirations. We are also "unschoolers" at times, especially when I see the school bus drive by our house in the morning and my heart fills with gratitude for the lives we have.

Our labels ebb and flow and grow. They change from day to day. In the end, labels are only words that could never describe the depth and breadth of everything our life embodies. When we got back from the Texas conference, Devin said that he missed our forest. (We live on 43 acres). He said he loved the city, but he wanted to create something out in nature.

So, today, Devin and I took on the task of making a lean-to, which is a shelter in the woods. He saw one on the show "Man vs. Wild" and has wanted to create one ever since. So we jumped online and researched how to do it. We gathered sticks together and created this interesting forest shelter.

This project was so much fun! I was in charge of tying everything together while he laid all of the sticks in the way he wanted. I love when he and I start building together. It takes me a few minutes to "get into it," but once I do, we are so in the moment and work together perfectly. We are supportive of one another, and if something isn't working, we encourage one another.

I love these times together. He loves that I am not afraid to "get dirty," in his words.

Yes, this might sound strange at first, but as the old saying goes, *Don't believe everything you think.* Children do not need to be forced to learn, ever. They *never* need to be punished, or motivated by grades to learn what they need in life to be successful and happy. Children never need to jump through the hoops, like most kids in our culture do, to get from point A to point B. **Open your eyes and see how brainwashed we truly are in our culture about what we think education and parenting are.** It's time to embrace the paradigm shift and evolve as a parent. Your children deserve it!

The true belief behind unschooling is...there is nothing that you cannot learn at home that you could learn in school...nothing. In fact, you can learn even more by spending your time pursuing your passions all day.

Most homeschoolers do school-at-home, meaning they buy a curriculum, they sit at the kitchen table and basically do what schools do. However, forced learning has negative repercussions, which include drastically affecting a child's self esteem and creating distaste for learning in general. If someone was forcing you to do something you did not enjoy, day in and day out against your will, would you ever find a joy in it? Or would you run anytime you were faced with something that remotely looked like learning?

My children chase their passions.

Unschooling philosophy suggests you trust your children in their ability to learn what they need in life, as they need it, by giving them the freedom that I feel all humans deserve. Learning through life is as natural as growing physically and emotionally. Reading, writing and math are all tools, very useful tools that our kids will pick up as we live a life surrounded by the written word and use numbers and math naturally everyday. What use would learning these things even be, if they weren't already part of lives?

Just like babies learn to walk and talk because these skills are useful tools to help them get what they want, so are the "basics" useful, desirable tools for our kids to get what *they* want in life. With this understanding we see that like a baby will learn

18

to walk and talk when they are ready, without ever needing classes, the same is true for older kids with skills like reading and writing. I know my children will learn all of the necessary skills and tools that they need for their own personal goals in life. I have always trusted that they would, and they have.

I see myself as their facilitator.

I do not look at myself as my children's teacher. I am not standing in front of them pouring knowledge into them as the *all-knowing* authority. My job is to give them as much of the world as possible from as many resources as possible so they learn and pursue their interests. My husband and I are present, by their side, to help them in any way that we can. Our roles are very involved and hands-on.

We do not have to know all the answers. In fact, if I were relying on what one person knew, like a teacher in a school, my own learning would be biased and limited. Living this unschooling life means we explore together because we don't know all the answers to every interest of everyone in the family.

We do however, know how to find all of the answers and this is what is most important. Through the Internet, television, books, video games, day trips, vacations, community resources, and apprenticeships, we offer our children more than traditional schooling could ever provide. We aren't afraid to say, *I don't know...let's learn about it together.*

Our kids are learning that answers aren't always black and white. They are learning about others' theories and philosophies and drawing their own answers and conclusions to the questions that all of us ponder. **In short, we are raising free-thinkers.**

Unschooling Moment: I Don't Have To Do It All

"Mom," Devin said, "I really want to learn how to play Pokemon."

"Okay," I said while thinking *I can't learn the rules of the game by reading about them. I have tried and just couldn't understand. The game seemed so complicated.* So what do I do?

I am his facilitator in his learning. I need to be able to do this, and I have no clue how to play Pokemon.

I tried to force myself to read how to play the game, but I felt like I was back in school trying to learn against my will. It just didn't feel good, and I was getting frustrated. But wait a moment! I didn't need to have all the answers. Nix that parenting thought! I needed to know how to find them for him. So I searched online. I found this interesting *Pokemon* tutorial video, which turned out to be a fun way for him to learn.

Devin thanked me for researching the many different ways to learn how to play Pokemon and finding the way that worked best for him. This is one of the many joys about living this life, having the freedom and time to find ways to facilitate learning in the best way.

Many people have asked me, "How do you know what your child is learning if your child is not in school, or you are not doing traditional school work and grading?" Well, how did you know when your child learned to walk or talk? You were there and witnessed the event, right? Unschooling holds the same viewpoint: I am by my children's side. I know what they learn. I am right with them, witnessing and participating. I do not need somebody else telling me what my children learn or sending home grades. I watch their learning unfold before me every day. Not only that, but **I believe that what my children are learning is their business, and it wouldn't feel right to be constantly prodding their minds to see what they know.** Again, I trust them and their learning process.

Education is not the *goal* of unschooling. Our goals are family connection and pursuing our interests together. Children do get an education as a side effect of living an abundant life together. Our home is filled with exciting, fun things to do like music, art, games and crafts. Our kitchen cabinets are filled with ingredients for cooking and for experiments. Our library overflows with interesting reading material, informative magazines, and intriguing games and puzzles. Most of all, we have *space*. Space to play, dance, create and explore. We have five televisions, four computers, handheld games, as well as many toys, including plastic and natural toys. Whatever our kids want, we strive to bring it into their lives.

Our children's *wants* are their *needs*.

Our environment is important to me as an Unschooling parent. I like to make sure there is always one large table clear at all times, so if someone wants to pull something out to explore or create, they can. My responsibility includes keeping things organized, and being involved and engaged with my children all day, everyday as well as pursuing my own interests and passions along side of them. I love this role and my children know that I am always there to look something up, read, or cook with them and to be utterly present as much as I can be.

The goal of unschooling is to help your child become who they are meant to be in life.

In our culture today, schools and education come first before family, fun, happiness, and pursuing our own interests. Children today are living others' agendas. This is sad to me. **Children are human beings who are living *now*.** Our cultural view of them is that they are always preparing for the future, always waiting to live instead of living now! Kids today are rarely given the opportunity to live now. Constantly preparing kids for the future is like adults having to sit in a classroom against their will all day, everyday, preparing for retirement. How fulfilling would our lives be?

I understand that we are well intentioned as a culture, but we are also making some big mistakes. Learning to live consciously and be aware in the **now**, rather than in a preparation for future living, changes everything. Living in the present is receiving more attention and value. Radical unschooling philosophy is extending this important understanding to children and families. This perspective on life is on the leading edge of thought, and is long overdue. **The time is now to take back**

22

your lives and the lives of your children and begin living a life of happiness. You can have it if you truly want it.

As an unschooling family, we put family first on the top of our priority list. We do not work our vacations around school breaks. We do not need to get *permission* from anyone to take our children where we want to take them. **We are living a life in the truest sense of freedom.**

Education happens and is an important part of life, but not before laying the solid, important foundation of trust, connection and joy of living together doing things you love as a family. We choose to put family first. I cannot imagine having to live our lives around a school's agenda and the demands the institution forces down the throats of parents. The schools' needs *always come before family needs*. This to me is utter madness and I choose not to have that be a part of our lives at all. **We live our lives together and our closeness as a family and our personal freedom is the most important thing to us.** Nothing comes before that.

Chapter Two

Mainstream Vs. Unschooling

If I had to make a general rule for living and working with children, it might be this: be wary of saying or doing anything to a child that you would not do to another adult, whose good opinion and affection you valued.

John Holt

In mainstream circles, people ask me questions about the children's homework or discipline, and I have to explain that radical unschooling doesn't function on some of the mainstream notions of those terms.

Our kids only have to finish as much or as little of what they're interested in. This aspect of natural learning is different than in a forced learning situation where children are not only forced to finish something, but are also graded on how well they do. The focus in not on content, just compliance and obedience.

The idea of *quitting* something doesn't exist in our lives because a child will complete as much as they want of a topic until they personally are satisfied. When they've gained enough knowledge or information, when their curiosity is complete, then they move on. Our children's work doesn't have to be finished or completed according to someone else's standards. **Unschooled kids can go as far as they**
24

can understand or desire, and this is a very personal choice, which isn't for anyone else to judge.

For example, my son Devin had drum lessons, and he has completed as much as he's felt necessary for his goals. He took a whole series of classes and then a couple more. He did not complete the second series because he felt he had learned what he wanted at that particular time. We bought him a drum set, which he plays for hours a day. When he reaches the point when his brain is ready for more, and he wants to, he may take lessons again. Maybe he will use an online tutorial or maybe choose to learn from a video. He learns everyday just by playing his drums. We trust and support him and offer him resources, but the choice is his. He never loses touch with his inner guidance in this way. **I love that we can give him this gift of confidence by never forcing, rewarding or coercing him.** We stay connected, and in turn he trusts and loves being around us, another positive side effect of living this philosophy.

Unschooling is such personalized education, one that no one else can tell you when you are done. **Learning never ends and we are never done.** We respect a child in their own path in what they want to know. The focus of radical unschooling is trust, freedom and the belief that humans learn best when they are internally motivated. When children are internally motivated, they will learn what they need to, and it will not be according to someone else's idea of what is best for them. *Learning is pleasurable when it isn't forced upon us.*

Also, kids in school are all being forced to learn the same things. Unschooled kids have as much knowledge as any child in school, but it is completely catered to their individuality. Our kids may not know the exact same things that a child in school does in certain areas, but in areas that are of interest to them, their knowledge *far exceeds* a child in school who has a "cookie-cutter" education. This rich, individualized knowledge is the epitome of a personalized education. **We are not all meant to know and learn the same things in life to be happy and succeed.**

Socialization

The socialization question comes up often living this life. There's no time in the life of an unschooled child where he or she is forced into a group of children their own age. That is a cultural practice of schools that we have been led to believe is the way children *should* spend their time. Nothing could be further from the truth. In the natural world, we never live in that scenario, all forced together with other 35 year olds, for example. Having children live in a classroom seven hours a day is very unnatural and affects their ability to connect with others who are *not* their own age. It actually disturbs the way humans are meant to socialize by nature.

Living this life includes interacting with all different people in our community from the bagger at the grocery store to the librarian to the people in the bakery. True socialization is being with people of all different ages and cultures, interacting, learning and sharing their lives together. My children do enjoy spending time with other kids, but none of them care about other kids' ages. They are focused on the

26

interests and hobbies of other kids. That is where connections happen. Connections matter! To connect and be forced into a situation where the only thing you have in common with someone is their age is pretty dull and leads to very unfulfilling relationships. Conflicts arise, and we learn that this is the way relationships are supposed to be. So we go on, never truly connecting with others who share our interests and beliefs. Dysfunction grows.

Unschooling Moment

Watching Dakota sparkle at the Rethinking Education Conference was amazing. She was totally herself and was embraced by everyone there. She and I were flipping through the conference schedule and noticed that there was a "Leonardo Da Vinci Invention Contest". I asked her if she would be interested, and she said, "Yes."

We walked down to the main floor and picked up our bag of invention materials. Everyone gets the exact same materials to create their invention with. Then conference attendees vote on 100 inventions and the winners from 3 categories get a prize.

Dakota created a "Barbie Doll Clothes Rack" on which to hang Barbie clothes. She did a great job creating her challenging invention. She wanted to win so badly.

The last night of the conference, they announced the winners of the contest. My heart swelled when they announced Dakota as the winner in the "Most Useful" category! She was so excited and shyly, but proudly, walked up on stage to claim her prize. Everyone clapped and cheered for her. I smile thinking of that special moment in her life.

Today she shares that winning the prize was one of her favorite things about the conference. It was so beautiful watching her up on stage... so proud... so confident.

Unschooled children's social skills are well rounded in that they interact and interface with a variety of people. We have friends whose children are in traditional schools as well as friends who have unschooled children. I've observed that kids who are unschooled and parented this way have no trouble walking up to an adult and starting a conversation.

The schooled children of my friends have a hard time even talking with me. They talk to other kids, but they don't ask me how I'm doing. Adults stand outside of their realm of experience except as an authority figure most of the time and not someone that they are comfortable speaking with, let alone befriending.

My son Devin sometimes visits a friend who lives down the street. He is just as close to this sixty five year old woman as he is to any friend his own age. He likes to be around her. He learns from her, whereas the average kid in school would not likely befriend an older woman. Devin would just as soon talk and make friends with a three year old as he would an eighty year old. I love that he has this internal freedom to use the rich pantry of people in our lives as potential friends based on their interests. How much bigger his world is than that of the average child. I am so happy that my children can choose from *anyone,* rather than follow the culturally conditioned ideas of choosing friends only from their age group in a limiting classroom setting.

Age segregation is not part of our real-world reality, which instead is more like a tribal life, where you're part of a huge community, resulting in a more natural, easy way to live. What better way for children to learn about diversity and acceptance!

28

Navigating Needs

One of my roles as an Unschooling Mom is making sure that everyone's needs are met and they feel listened to. For example, if the kids are arguing over a game or a book, they might ask me to be the voice to communicate differences or to navigate between them. Another example would be if somebody is screaming at the other one, I might take a deep breath and calmly share, *Devin really wanted to have a turn with that game. How long do you need before you're finished?* I can be be the voice of calmness in helping them navigate conflict. **Finding win/win situations for my children is all part of my days with them.**

Household Functioning

When I gather with other parents at Unschooling conferences, much discussion takes place around how our households handle tasks like meal times, bed times and chores. Another big issue is television viewing and limits. These are issues on the minds of parents who are coming to understand this life.

In our household, these common issues are not problems or difficulties. We totally trust our children's needs: they go to bed when they're tired and wake up when they're rested, just like we do. They watch as much television or play as many video games as they like.

Upon hearing that, some parents would say that was crazy, and think that children would watch TV and play video games non-stop. Yet they don't. They have such a wonderful balance because they have the freedom to choose. Also, kids in school use television in a much different way than our unschooled kids. Kids in school often use it as a tool to decompress and to escape their reality. Our kids use television as a tool for learning and a way to see more of the options in our world by seeing true human potential. They use it as a learning tool and a way to pursue more of their interests. All of the studies conducted of television use and its harmful effects have been done on schooled children, not unschooled kids who use television with totally different intentions. Such studies do not apply to our kids.

Bedtimes

In our household our younger children Ivy and Orion go to bed around nine or ten. We usually have baths and read stories and cuddle. Bedtime is something pleasurable to them. My older kids, Devin and Dakota, stay up and watch television, play games or read books. They usually get tired and go to bed around eleven or midnight. We have never experienced bedtimes to be challenging, any more than it would be for us as adults. I enjoy going to sleep and so do my children - when we are tired and ready.

In the winter we stay up a lot later. In the summer we go to bed earlier; it's a natural ebb and flow of their internal clocks which change with the seasons. This is not only a more joyful way to live, but also a much healthier one. We are meant to ebb and flow with the seasons. We are, after all, part of the earth's rhythms. **Honoring these natural rhythms is one of the benefits living a radical unschooling life.**
30

We don't have a time schedule, but we have a rhythm to our evenings. We usually have dinner together and then play games, read or watch a show. Right now, Joe is over in our playroom above his workshop playing with the kids. They're playing wrestling games and tag and throwing balls around. When they come back, they'll be ready to unwind, put on their pajamas and have a snack. This is a pretty average evening for us. **We may not live by a schedule like most people, but we have a rhythm to our life that fluctuates to meet everyone's needs from day to day**.

Unschooling Moment

Pushing through fear and moving toward trust is an important aspect of this life we choose to live with our kids. Most of us were raised in a time in human history where we were controlled by fear-inducing tactics from teachers and caregivers. The worst-case scenarios were forced on us, and we did what someone else wanted because we were afraid of the punitive consequences. Think back, I know you can remember just a few instances when this was true.

Fear is a tool used to motivate others to do what you want - and it works well in doing just that! Mainstream parenting promotes this "tool" to control our kids to meet our needs. Kids believe what their parents say and treat their words as fact. The words are paired with fear and become their neuro-associations, forevermore a part of them.

Using fear as a motivational tool has life-altering side effects. This is why I choose to move away from such tactics with my own children. It takes work and effort to get over the fears instilled in us when we were children.

I thought of posting this as the girls were making breakfast this morning. I had those knee-jerk worst case scenario fears whispering at me for the first few minutes of them using very hot pans, but I told that voice to shut up so I could allow the voice of *Trust* to sing to me. Do you know the side effect of trust rather than fear?

Meal Times

For dinner, I might provide a small buffet that includes something everybody likes. I don't ever force my kids to eat something they don't like, nor do I force them to sit at dinner with us. They can sit and watch television or go in the other room. They usually want to be with us however, because when you lead this life, your kids *want* to be around you. **Our kids really like us**, and meal times are usually spent together because it is pleasurable, never forced with threats of punishments.

When our kids sit down with Joe and I for dinner, it is because they want to be with us and eating together is a family event. If dinner is ready and someone is in the middle of something, I offer to bring their food out to them. My kids really appreciate this.

Chores

Our kids do not have "chores". They do however, joyfully help out around the house. Devin likes to vacuum and Dakota and Ivy like to dust and clean windows and sweep the kitchen. Our kids clean because *it makes sense to do so*. They enjoy being part of this aspect of our family living. I never make them clean their rooms either. I take the responsibility to keep their rooms clean because I know that if I provide them with models of clean, organized space, they will get used to having it that way and keep up with it as they get older.

Devin will ask me to help him reorganize his room or help him clean it and I am so happy to do it for him. He feels most comfortable with his room and our home organized and clean. All of the kids do, and I feel that it is my responsibility to offer this to my family. To be clear, cleanliness it isn't a need of mine, and never comes before the needs of my kids. A clean home is simply a balancing act and I do bits and pieces throughout the day. Joe and the kids all take part in keeping up our home. If they see something that needs to be done, they usually just do it, if they are able. I believe this is because I do housework joyfully and in gratitude for our home and the lives we live. I can not imagine that my kids would help out so much if every time I cleaned I complained about the "mess". It is important for me that our home be a cozy nest filled with joyful activities and relaxing nooks. I want our home to be the place that my family wants to be more than anywhere else in the world, and I am proud to say that it is.

Kindness

I am kind to my children as I talk to them and in the way that treat them. Much of traditional parenting is replete with critical overtones, even though most parents do not see it that way. When you are kind to your kids, they learn kindness to others.

When you punish them and treat them coercively, they learn to be mean to others and to you. It is so simple, yet so complicated for most parents to grasp. Kindness begets kindness. Respect begets respect. **Children learn what they live and we take this very seriously and very literally.**

Imagine guests are visiting your home. How would you treat them as a gracious host or hostess? What kind of respect would you afford your guests? You'd likely say, *Hey, you know, dinner is at seven. We'd love for you to join us. If you don't like what we have to offer, I'd be happy to make you something else.*

I would never say to a guest, *Dinner's ready! Come sit down and be still. If you are not, you have to go sit in the naughty-guest spot. Also, you need to clean your plate or no dessert for you.* What kind of relationship would we have if we treated a guest that way? What effect does it have on your child? Think about it.

Living with respect for children does take some time. You need to rewire your brain to stop seeing that kids are people who need to be trained and learn to see them as people who deserve the same kindness and respect that we would give our guests, or friends, or anyone else whom we value in our lives.

Parents lose touch with their instinctual wisdom, their natural awareness, by being brought up in the way most of us have. Parenting today looks so much more like dog training than raising a human being. The focus on obedience is causing disconnection and damage that I know people feel. I see the pain and confusion in the parents' eyes on "Nanny 911" and I want to reach into the television and hug them and share that there is another way, a better way. I want to share that the pain they feel is their internal guidance letting them know that what they are doing through punishing their kids and demanding obedience goes against who they are and what they know instinctually.

One of my goals and dreams in life is to have a new and differing show, much like "Nanny 911", where I can go into people's homes and help them resolve problems with this respectful, peaceful parenting philosophy. I know it will happen when everything lines up for me to do so. I plan to call the show, "Radical Resolutions."

Parents today are doing the best they can with what they know, parenting as a function of how they were raised. Yet, they are feeling empty and wondering why their kids do not like them or want to be around them. We hear catch words like, "rebellion" and chalk it up to normalcy, but what if there was nothing to rebel against? **What if we lived the respect for our children that we demand they have for us?** What if we could recognize that punishments always model meanness, that use of power should never be violent, and when children learn this from us they are learning to be harsh and violent themselves?

What if we opened our eyes and saw all that could be by choosing to evolve as parents, and learned another way? Radical unschooling is this other way and provides the answers to many of today's problems that parents face with their children. Unschooling families do not deal with "rebellion" because we are never the wall standing between our kids and their wants. In fact we see our role as helping our children get what they want in life. We facilitate them on this path to their desires. We move from power struggles and control to connection and true, respectful family relationships. **When we make this shift, we discover the love and deep feelings of joy that we are meant to have by nature as parents.**

Sometimes, I imagine myself as an anthropologist when I sit at a playground or museum. I sit back and watch how people are with their kids. I observe that their interactions with children are very different than the way they interact with the average (adult) person. They're constantly training: *good job, bad job, don't do that, do this.* This constant giving of information and judgment about how their kids act at every single moment is an unnatural way to interact with another human being whom you value and love. It is exhausting and not pleasurable for either parent or child. Why do most parents do this? Because it is all they know, until now.

Anytime we try to control another, we can't connect with true joy. It feels very different for me to be around someone practicing "mainstream parenting" and training their child vs. being with their child in the present moment and flowing with them in a relaxed, natural way, interacting with their child lovingly and kindly.

Mainstream parenting has to do with a fear-of-the-future based living vs. being utterly present. There's a huge distinction between the two viewpoints and contrasting ways of living with our children. People do not see training a child as being unkind, but it's very frustrating for the child to be judged constantly. I know. I lived that way. You lived that way. Most of us were raised in that manner. We

36

know what it felt like to be judged, continuously evaluated and punished for not being obedient. It never felt good, but we never knew any differently.

We grew up carrying anger, judgment and intolerance for others because those raising us were trained to believe that they needed to demand obedience and have their own needs met at the sacrifice of their children's needs. Thank goodness we are now learning where we went wrong and how we can do better!

I know there are always going to be those who choose mainstream values, but I want to show you an alternative, holistic approach that is making history and changing the way that many people view their roles as parents. This evolved approach to parenting is respectful, being present, modeling and living in a way that we know our children will grow to be with others. It wholly embraces the idea that **children learn what they live.**

Chapter Three

Basic Unschooling Values

You did then what you knew how to do.

When you knew better, you did better.

Maya Angelou

Basic Value System

Radical unschooling is an extension of my natural birthing and bonding days of developing a connection with my children through attachment. Attachment parenting has to do with trusting our children and being responsive to their needs. In fact, trust is the basis for the unschooling life.

- I trust that when my baby cries, he needs to be held.

- I trust that when my baby wants to be with me at night, that she should be by my side, in bed with us.

- I trust that when my child wants to eat, he will let me know and I will feed him as often and for as long as he needs.

I do not feel that I know better than my children do when it comes to their own wants and needs. Traditional parenting believes that children are manipulative. This idea and belief causes much distrust in the parent/child relationship. I have never viewed my children in this way. Trust has always been the backdrop of our lives together. When you tune in to your instinctual wisdom and silence the voices that think they know better than your intuitive self, it becomes easier and more joyful to connect with your children.

We do not focus on our children's "behavior." We focus on their needs underlying the behavior. That's a huge shift in philosophy from traditional control issues. Where traditional parenting focuses solely on behavior, the connection model looks at what need is not being met and places the focus where it belongs - on the need. I also understand that I have had years of experience in learning to control my screaming, hitting and physical forms of frustration, and my children have not yet learned to control those impulses. Hitting is a form of communication for young children. I know that they are doing the best that they can with what they know. I always assume the best of intent rather than the worst, which is a culturally negative way to view children.

In reality, when two and three year olds throw things, what is underneath the behavior? A real need? Are they simply playing? How can you as a parent meet their need in a kind and loving way?

Mainstream parenting would focus on the behavior and may say: *that's bad, don't do that, and if you do that again you're sitting on the naughty step, or will have your toy taken away.* Unschooling philosophy would ask: *okay, this child has a need to throw things and how can we meet that need?* I might say: *okay sweetie, here's a softer ball, or here's a stuffed animal, or let's go outside and throw this around where nothing will get broken.* I would find a way to meet the need, that basic primitive biological need to throw things, vs. focusing on training the behavior or punishing for it. Which approach feels better, lighter and more connected, and which way feels disconnected and painful?

This is a huge paradigm shift for most parents. It can be mind-blowing and empowering the first time one understands how traditional parenting focuses on the parent's needs and not the child's. When you first learn about this, your mind expands and you begin to see the possibilities for a deeper, more respectful connection with your child. You begin to see them as equals and realize that punitive methods are not very kind or productive. You may cry as you learn about this and feel pain and guilt. This is all normal. You will soon work through these feelings and start a whole new chapter of your life together as parent and child. Gratitude will fill your heart and you will be on this new road, hand in hand with your children, with confidence.

Unschooling Moment

Devin told me last week that he wanted to take gymnastics. I found a class and signed him up. Yesterday was his first class. He was so excited! When we got there, he walked right up to the teacher, stuck out his arm for a handshake and said, "Hi, My name is Devin Martin." The teacher looked so surprised. She introduced herself and Devin said, "Nice to meet you." I laughed to myself when I saw the teacher was in awe that he was so confident in new situations.

The class started with stretches and led into forward and backward rolls, then handstands, then work on the balance beam. It looked so amazing and so fun! We were walking to the car and I asked, "So... how'd you like your first class babe?" He said, "I hated it! It was lame and boring and not at all what I thought".

Now, the beauty of living a respectful and connected life with our kids means also living in non-judgment. It was fine with me that he didn't want to go back. We don't live by someone else's standards that we need to "finish what we start." We *do* finish what we start, but it is on our own terms. We are finished when we are done. Period.

Also, I hear so often that parents make their kids stay in classes where they are not happy because of money spent, where there is usually a way to get refunds or roll the money over into another class. Money would never be a reason why I would make my child stay in a class where they weren't happy. My kids' feelings are more important than money.

I saw this as such a great thing! Devin tried something new and learned that he didn't want to do it again. But the cooler thing still was that on the way in to gymnastics class, Devin saw an enormous climbing wall and said, "I want to do that!" We never would have known about that wonderful new hook for him had he not taken the gymnastics class.

To me, this life is about offering our children a rich buffet of options and activities for their learning. They joyfully take what appeals to them. There is no retribution for stopping classes or projects. There is only pure, authentic freedom without guilt, coercion, or shame. There are authentic choices with no strings attached.

As Devin and I hung out in bed last night talking, I asked him if he wished he never went to gymnastics class. He replied, "No. It was boring, but I learned how to do a handstand and a backward roll. I learned what I wanted, now it's time to learn how to climb!"

We are off on another adventure and it feels good to all of us! Life is what you create and choose to see in any given situation. We choose to create happiness, understanding and connection in all that we do, and I am so grateful for that!

Watching Television

I was asked once if I'd let my toddler watch television even though the American Pediatric Association advises against it for kids less than two years old. My answer to that question focused on the fact that there's a big difference between the television serving as a child's babysitter vs. a parent watching their favorite shows *with* them. Being present with children, talking about the shows, sitting and cuddling while you watch together, is just another way to connect in the same way as reading a book, just following your child's interests.

The whole act of watching a television show is very different with a clear intention behind it. For example, my daughter Dakota loves Hannah Montana. To honor her passion, I have become her partner in this interest in every way. I mark on the calendar when the show is on. We all watch together, laugh and enjoy what she has introduced us to. We recently bought her the Hannah Montana video game and poster for her room. She thanked us for these things, and she knows we will be there to help fuel her passions in life, whatever they may be.

I love the *Food Network*. I know that I value learning through television as much as I value learning through books. Learning is learning, no matter what medium we use to obtain it. **I do not judge the value of what my kids learn, whether from a book, television or through a video game.**

Devin loves the show *Man Vs. Wild*. Through watching, he has learned so much about survival in the wilderness, and it has sparked a desire to learn even more about the topic. If I only allowed my son to learn about his interests through books, he may never have been introduced to the topic.

When a parent is opposed to something like their child watching television, it creates a power struggle between parent and child. The child will try to become powerful by watching more television or demanding more of an activity because he's afraid that it's going to be taken away from him. He soon learns to not trust his parent, and soon after, the issue is no longer about the show, or whatever it is they are wanting. It transforms from a desire for something to a struggle for autonomy and free will. The power struggle distorts the situation so much that a child loses touch with their true desires. This warping of desire and behavior creates an unnatural overuse of the initial desire, be it food, television or video games, for example. **Once you let go of the power struggle and become your child's partner, a child can have his desire met, respectfully, naturally and with balance.**

The World is a Joyful Place

It took a real shift to see my child's joy and passion outweigh my own agenda and fear as a new mom. I had read a popular magazine for mothers about protecting my child from the evils of media, an age-old social concern. The perpetuation of the message portrayed my child as the victim of the evil advertisers vying for his attention. This way of thinking is not the way I want to share the world with my son. Our world is not an evil place waiting to snatch his innocence. It is a place of beauty, love and abundance. **I want my children to know what an incredibly beautiful world they live in, not a bad fearful place where they need to be cautious at every step.**

There are two primary emotions in life with regard to interacting with our children. One is love and the other is fear. When I lapse into fear, life seems scary. Parenting seems overwhelming. When I become more selective by bringing into my life that which solidifies my knowing that we live in a wonderful world, filled with great things for our family, parenting feels better, lighter and joyful. I shift from a fear-based mindset to a more trusting, open mindset.

If you can view the world as evil or good, and we know that there is just as much of each, why choose to focus on the negative, bad things out there? What are our children learning from this way of being in the world? Which feels better - love or fear - to share with your child? This decision is totally personal, and you can ask yourself: *How can I choose to live in gratitude and joy today for the world we live in?*

At conferences, we have had great discussions with other parents about fears surrounding the media's impact on children. At the same time, I believe that children are human beings just as we are. My husband likes horror movies. I am not fearful that he is going to go on a chainsaw rampage because he watched a movie which was violent.

I understand that there is a primitive human curiosity to learn about and see violence, fighting and sex. It is normal to slow down on the highway and stare at car accidents. Does this mean that we are going to cause one because we are interested? No, we are fulfilling a need and that isn't wrong or negative. It is part of all of us. We are curious creatures. **I would rather my children have me at their sides explaining things, rather than forbidding their curiosity.**

Challenge your long-held beliefs about parenting, and you'll find many that are not true. Tap into your instinctual wisdom as our children are naturally tapping into theirs. **Don't warp their inner knowing by not tuning into yours.**

Everyone is doing the best they can,
with what they know at the time.

Our Contribution To The World

There was a period about ten years ago when I boycotted Nestle. I used to be so angry with Nestle for what they were doing by marketing infant formula to third world countries. I took the boycott very seriously and held on to much frustration and anger about the boycott. I warned others and emailed angry protesting emails about how everyone should join me in the fight against them. One day, I had a profound realization.

I came to see that I was not contributing to the peace of the world by holding on to these strong negative emotions. My children were being affected. I was contributing to the negativity of the world through my thoughts and my angry actions and feelings.

I changed my thoughts and actions to focus on what was working with the world. I pledged: *I am going to focus more on breastfeeding awareness and helping women with breastfeeding difficulties, as opposed to being anti-formula, or anti anything for that matter.* This was a huge shift in thinking for me and it has spiraled me upward to release any kind of "anti" mindset that I had about anything in the past. This has not only benefited me as a person, but everyone I come in contact with.

> *Mother Teresa said, "If you ever have an anti-war rally, do not invite me, but if you have a march for peace, I will be there."*

Reading her statement is profound. When you are against something, you feed into it, and it grows in your consciousness. The energy you are putting forth is always adding to what you are focused on, regardless if you are for or against something.

Contributing to peace and what I believe in and stand for, rather than butting up against what I *don't* believe in or value, has been one of the keys to my happiness in life. I no longer judge others for their choices when they are not in alignment with my own. I know that everyone is doing the best they can with who they are and with what they know.

First and foremost is our connection with our kids
and meeting them where they are.

Our children learn how to be in this world by watching how we live our lives. I want my children to feel safe in their world and know that they can pursue their dreams with confidence. I do not believe that we live in a big, bad world just waiting to victimize my children and myself. I believe in the good of others and all that is working in the world. I know that my thoughts become my reality and how I choose to view the world is such a key factor to a life of happiness and wholeness for my children and myself.

When you approach living and learning in a passionate, joyful way, children learn to be peaceful and trusting. **They become partners with the world and see endless possibilities and choices surrounding them.** They see the beauty in themselves and others.

Chapter Four

Nurture Your Child's Passions

All you need is passion.

If you have a passion for something, you'll create the talent.

Yanni

One child may love ninjas or fighting characters. Maybe she dresses in black, dies her hair red and sings heavy metal songs. Why does one parent fear it and another joyfully embrace her daughter's choices?

Children do not judge their interests as bad or dark things. Rather, they are being true to themselves. I speak from my own experience of loving heavy metal music from the age of 13. I loved bands such as *Metallica* and *Obituary*. I loved anything with a strong, fast, heavy rhythm. I played guitar and spent most of my free time with friends that formed a heavy metal band.

It was such an incredible passion and one that was viewed as corrupt and evil by others in my life. I never thought of my passion as evil, but through others thinking so, I was changed. I began disliking myself, afterall how could I like something that others thought was so bad? In being true to myself, I lost connection to those in my life that I cared about and who cared about me. I lost my inner knowing of my own goodness. Their fear distorted who I was.

Our kids have passions and curiosities; they might share our interests or not. Classical music makes me cry; it is depressing to me. I cannot listen to slow country music either for the same reason. Forget it. Heavy metal and hip hop music are joyful to me because it speaks to me energetically. It always has.

Devin loves Latin music. It is important for me to introduce my children to every kind of music available, even if I do not care for it. I want them to have the freedom to choose from the whole wide world of musical expression out there. Latin music is what spoke to him the most of all that he heard a few years ago. Since that time his musical tastes have expanded. He still enjoys Latin music, and it was a doorway for his current interest in Latin history and foods. **Any interest is of value, even if you don't understand it at first.** Many times small nuggets of interest are enormous springboards into a whole new world or experience.

Unschooling presents the opportunity of honoring
where everybody is and not judging it.

To honor our children's passions, we parents can do two things:

1. Celebrate our *own* passions and let our children see that learning never ends. Rekindle your flames of curiosity and interest in the world. Explore for the sake of your own enjoyment of learning.

2. Move through any of our past associations that cause us to project our fears on our kids.

A lot of times we see things and instantly our brain will connect to an image or feeling in our past. School shootings on television might be a reactionary place for us. When we see a gun, we might think of that. Video game violence might remind us of gang shootings we witnessed in the media, for example.

So it is important to recognize, separate out that reaction and ask ourselves: *Why do I feel this way?* On this unschooling journey, my parenting has involved a lot of internal dialogue and searching: *Why am I feeling bad about certain things my kids are showing an interest in? Was it the way I was raised? Was it associations with past events?*

Our parenting reactions are coming from a purely innocent place.

To nourish and support children's passions, radical unschooling philosophy holds certain perspectives you may find helpful.

- First, we want to value our children's needs as much as we do our own needs.

- Secondly, we can strive to be utterly present with our children, and move from the fear of the future mindset in which traditional parenting is often based in.

- Thirdly, we want to infuse our family lives with respect and kindness because we know that children learn what they live. The whole *Do As I Say Not As I Do* parenting methods of the past have proven to be disastrous to both the parent-child relationship, the child's self-esteem, and our culture as a whole.

Unschooling Moment

Thinking outside the box takes on many forms in our lives. Once you start thinking free it picks up momentum until it saturates your whole life. You begin to question everything and say "Why not?" more often. A new way of life opens to create, dream, imagine and look at things through an entirely different lens.

We love to create new games together as a family. We also love to play around and alter the rules of games like Candyland, bowling, mini golf...you name it, we've made the rules more cooperative or more competitive, depending on the day and our whims.

Today the kids were asking me why hopscotch only has one basic design layout. Dakota suggested making a circle or spiral for hopscotch. I thought it was an amazing idea! Devin helped me draw out the design.

There is so much that our children learn through living a full, peaceful, interest-driven life. This morning we woke up not knowing what we were going to do for the day. (I love this about our lives - we create life as we go, and rarely do we have appointments or plans that cannot be changed.) We often call friends to come on adventures with us and have so much fun, only guided by the moment on most days. It really is a blissful life together.

This morning Dakota said she wanted to have a lemonade stand. Sounded great to me! We have never had one before and all the kids got excited about. We had the lemonade ingredients and we just needed a pitcher and some cups. We went to a grocery store and got everything we needed.

We made signs which Joe hammered into the ground. I set up a blanket nearby and hung out with Orion and read to him while the kids waited for their first customer. While we set up, the kids and I discussed how to greet people, how to serve the lemonade, how to make change and all the little details of having their own "business."

Their first customer stopped and the kids jumped out of their seats. Devin greeted them with, "How are you doing today?" and Dakota ended with a, "Would you like a slice of lemon in your lemonade?" The cars stopped every couple of minutes. Who can resist three adorable kids sitting behind a lemonade stand waving as they drive by? They absolutely blew my mind. I am still in awe of how well they handled everything! I didn't know what to expect, but they were confident, positive and so friendly to everyone!

They made $23.00 in less than 3 hours! Almost everyone told them to keep the change and gave them tips for great service! It was one of those days when I see how incredible this unschooling life actually is. I got a glimpse into all that they already knew about running a business. It was remarkable to see all that they have learned through immersion, watching and learning from us as we operate our own home businesses.

Trusting kids to learn really works. You never have to force a child to learn anything, really....you don't. Kids can't help learning when they have a rich, full, exciting life together with involved parents.

Yup....the Martin kids learned so much today, as they do everyday...I just got to see it loud and clear today in such a unique way! It was an experience that brought me further up the ladder of trust and understanding of how well a respectful, free life is in preparing my kids for the future, even though we don't think about that much. We focus on living in the moment most of the time.

They worked out their roles as they were waiting for customers. Devin handled the money while Dakota served everyone. It was fun helping them understand good customer service and sanitary ways to serve customers. The kids saw themselves as strong, capable and intelligent. They grew so much today from a simple lemonade stand! They learned about the art of entrepreneuring and it felt so good to help them on this path!

The lemonade is chilling in the fridge for tomorrow... The kids can't wait for their second day with their very own money-making business!

Tomorrow is going to be a good day.... as usual.

Focus on What is Working

You put your focus what you see and attract. I choose to see the joy, wonder, beauty and peace of everything that is working in this world. There is just as much that is working as isn't working. You can choose to focus and get pulled in and drown in a deep, dark, awful place. Or, you can rise up and choose to see all that is wonderful. You always have a choice.

Children see their passions as extensions of themselves. If you are approaching their interests from a negative place, implying, *That stuff is bad. That is violent,* their brain translates our opinion into this: *There is something wrong with me for liking this thing that Mom thinks is bad. There must be something wrong with me.*

Children internalize our feelings and opinions about them.

With a solid foundation of trust and connection, our children are going to excel. They are securely attached to us, which is the healthy, normal way that humans are designed to be. When a child is securely attached, they have us totally - body, mind, and spirit - to be there for them. There is nothing more important than secure attachment and a solid foundation of love and trust between parent and child. To think that memorizing spelling words is better preparation for a child's future than a strong family connection of trust is utter nonsense.

Ninety percent of the kids in the world today are saying,
"I am not securely attached. I need something. I need something."

Meeting Kid's Needs

The radical unschooling life means finding win/win situations when conflicts arise and needs clash. Discussion and clear communication between everyone who has needs in the family are our goals.

There are never power struggles because everyone's needs are of value, even those of my one-year- old son. Orion has his needs met simultaneously as everyone else in our family. My children expect this and have lived this way since they were born. If Orion is crying, they will pick him up. If Ivy, my four year old, wants to play on the computer, they work together and come up with solutions. Just tonight I heard Devin telling Dakota that he would play for an hour, and then she could. He asked what she thought and she said, "No. How about half and hour?" They agreed. They know that finding win/win situations is part of living a peaceful, happy life together. It is their default way of being.

The traditional authoritarian parenting paradigm of solely meeting the parents' needs, as marketed by the media, books, and on shows like "Nanny 911", are the norm in our culture. People coming to this way of life from the norm think that the pendulum must swing all the way in the other direction of being devoted to meeting the child's needs only. Not so! Parents have needs, too. This is a big reason why I have heard parents say, "Unschooling didn't work for our family."

All that most parents know is by-control ruling rather than balancing and respecting equally the needs of everyone in the family. These parents surrender their own needs, in place of running around to meet the demands of their children only. Not only does this make for an unhappy parent, but the child learns that her parents view their own needs as secondary to their own needs. That isn't what this life is all about!

When parents misunderstand the philosophy they burn out quickly and in doing so give up, believing mistakenly that what they just experienced was "unschooling". In reality, they were only half way here!

We live in that wonderfully balanced place where parents' needs and children's needs are met in harmony. I look at our lives as a microcosm of world peace. Living this life means we are modeling how it is possible to respect others with different beliefs, values and interests without judgment. I can think of no better way to live life along side of our children in such an authentic way.

By living in harmony with our children we are:

- Embracing

- Surrendering

- Stepping out of any power struggle

- Meeting in the middle

I like to think of my family's life together as a river. My kids are the rocks in the river, and I am the water that flows around the rocks. I have the life experience of patience and flexibility to meet my own needs before, after and during the time when I am helping them to meet theirs. It is my responsibility to ensure I meet my own needs, rather than expecting my children to do so.

Chapter Five

Embracing & Honoring

Take the hand of your child and invite her to go out and sit with you on the grass.

The two of you may want to contemplate the green grass,

the little flowers that grow among the grasses, and the sky.

Breathing and smiling together - that is peace education.

If we know how to appreciate these beautiful things,

we will not have to search for anything else.

Peace is available in every moment, in every breath, in every step.

Thich Nhat Hanh

Have you ever had the need to vent to your partner? You go on, and all of a sudden, your partner is trying to fix it for you? They start lecturing you or offering solutions, and you feel like, *This is not what I need right now. I just want to be heard.*

Children are no different than we are in their desire to be heard, not "fixed". Often times we think as a traditional, mainstream parent because we were raised that way. That is, we hold a view of training our kids - similar to dog training - instead of honoring who they are and becoming their partners in life. From the trainer's viewpoint, everything in mainstream is the opportunity to tell children how they *should* be.

Dad, I am really afraid.

Well, you know, if you did not do this and you did not watch that, then you would not feel this way. This feels like shaming and can create a wall between parent and child. After such a comment a child may decide not to share his feelings again because of the negative reaction to his fears.

How about an alternative: *Do you need a hug? I know hugs sometimes make me feel safe.*

Partnering with your child can be so pure and straightforward, without the hidden agenda of *fixing* them. You could also say, *I can tell that scared you sweetie. Do you want to talk about it?* Validating and reflecting back what you think your child experienced is often all that is needed. Doesn't it feel good to be heard and validated? Our kids are no different.

You do not have to take every single opportunity, out of fear for their future, to tell children what you perceived they did wrong. Instead, you can come from a joyful, pure, honest, totally-in-the-present moment of saying: *That is a bummer. I'm sorry that happened to you.* Then offer a smile or a hug.

Changing Interests

So you discover what your child's passion is, and then it changes. As children grow older, however, you may find a common theme among their interests. You might notice a connection to nature, a curiosity about stars and the universe, an obsession with horses, or an exploration in how machines work, or a fascination with building structures.

When parents see these changing interests, they wonder, *How do I support my child's passion, provide resources without taking over, invading space or forcing their learning in another direction?* The question is an important issue for parents who are committed to living a free, joyful life with their children. I know what these parents are asking. They may have made a huge investment of their time and effort into one of their child's projects, only to discover their daughter's fairy princess stage has changed into playing a new online game. Here is what I've learned:

- Not every interest is going to be a passion. Some interests last days, some years.

- Like the river, go with the natural flow of their interests.

- Stay connected and do not try to control their choices.

- When you see that it might be going in another direction, release any attachment to a particular outcome and be with them. Trust where their new passion is guiding them.

My son was interested in Egyptian pharaohs. I jumped online and researched local museums. I found an interesting pharaoh museum, and the pharaoh exhibit was coming to the Boston Museum of Science. I found magazines having to do with Egypt, and asked, "Would you like to check those out?" He picked the one that he wanted and we ordered it. Next, his passion was to travel to Egypt, and I suggested, "Well, why don't we go on YouTube.com and check out the many cool videos of Egypt." We sat together, him in my lap, connecting and discussing for a long time. He bounced ideas off of me and we talked about what we were learning together.

All you have to do is go with the natural flow of the interests and learning and offer as many resources as you can to bring more of their interests into their lives to expand upon. I get excited when my kids have a new interest, because I love discovering resources with them. Magazines, websites, online videos, movies, games, exhibits, books, hands-on experiences and discussions are all of my children's learning tools.

We get a magazine subscription for my daughter called *Sparkle World*. It is all about Polly Pockets, Strawberry Shortcake, and such characters that she loves. I have friends who think that I am buying into commercialism. There is an entire school of thought that feels pop culture is damaging. What I feel is damaging is living in fear, following someone else's ideas and agendas of what is destructive and applying it to your own life without questioning whether it is true for you. I choose to trust my daughter's natural curiosities, rather than buy into protecting her from the "evils" of what others view as commercialism. **I trust what she is drawn to and know that if something makes her shine, it can only be good for her**.
60

I know that any time I place limits on what interests my children and motivates their learning, I am limiting their choices and options of what is available in the smorgasbord of life. **The most organic, natural way for me to live with my children is to trust them in their interests and choices.** I know that learning is everywhere, even in the places that others choose to control and keep from their kids. **When we limit or forbid something, we are limiting potential learning and growth experiences.**

Passions Go Through Cycles

On my mothering journey, gems and minerals fascinated me at a time when my children studied them. We shared that passion. When their interests shifted to *Sponge Bob*, it initially took time for me to value the topic as much as I valued their interests in gems and minerals. Once I let go of the fear associated with their love of *Sponge Bob*, a shroud lifted from my eyes. I saw how much they learned from the show. Discussions that stemmed from the show included oceanography, personal relations, fast food vs. whole foods. Most of all, the unconditional love that Sponge Bob shows his friend is admirable. When I pushed through the fear to trust, I saw what my children saw, and this became a perfect example for me of how love leads to learning and how fear stunts personal growth.

Valuing what my children were drawn to, no matter how much others frowned upon it, was a huge shift and source of enlightenment for me. Now I will tell anyone what my children's interests are, because they are all equally valid in my eyes. I am proud of any interest they have, as it is an extension of my children themselves.

There are no limits, no boundaries. **The entire world exists for us to learn and grow from.**

Unschooling Moment

I speak a lot about *internal motivation* being what drives an individual to learn, not someone else's agenda for that person. This one aspect of Unschooling seems hard for people to understand and surrender to because it requires so much trust in our children.

Unschooling is an amazing balance of "being there" with our kids to observe and notice when that internal motivation is kicking in. Then, how do we facilitate and help our kids feed that internal motivation? Without both parts of the "whole," the child is being neglected in his wanting to learn *more*. We need to be there as active, involved parents - not to lead.. - but *to assist, to offer, to respect* when we need to take a step back also. My children honestly and purely let us know what they need. It is my job to *listen* and "be there" by their side and to facilitate their learning.

I don't mean to just be there physically. For me to "be there" means to be emotionally tuned in, so that I see their internal motivation shining like a bright light, informing me that it is time to offer support and encouragement.

A lot of talk in mainstream parenting focuses on the belief that there is a rare "window of opportunity" in which a child is ready to learn certain skills. It is presented to us as specific, vital times in a child's life with arbitrary dates and ages. It makes learning seems technical, mysterious and difficult. We are told that if we miss these vital "windows" that our children will never learn certain things. We are told that we need to force feed this information to our children over and over again until they get it. I do not buy into this belief, because personal experience has shown me how false it is.

I know when my children are ready to learn something new because *they tell me. They show me.* I know because I am here, present and connected. I know *exactly* when those "window's of opportunity" are open because I am with them everyday. I do not need to have someone else tell me when they are ready to learn certain things. It isn't as complicated as we are led to believe. It is truly easy....Joyful....and fun because we go with the flow of learning and it is an organic, natural process that is supposed to feel good. It *does* feel good, we are living proof!

Ivy saw me making a grocery list and wanted to make one too. She said, "Mom, how do I draw those?"

Do you mean letters?"

"Yeah, letters." she said. "I want to make a list too".

I sat with her for a while, but she wasn't into *me showing her* how to do it. She wanted total independence in her exploration, but she was frustrated because she didn't know where to begin. I brainstormed for a few minutes on what I could offer her that would help her on this path. I remembered the cool *Leap Frog* letter toys for the fridge that tells you the letter and sound.

Wow....did she love this! She sat for a long time listening to different letter sounds. I showed her one way she could hold her pen. Then she began copying the letters onto paper. She was *writing letters*! It was amazing! She made herself a grocery list and brought it with us. At the store she kept showing me what she "needed" at the store. "Oh....you need a "K" Ivy! Great!" She is such a unique learner. I joyfully facilitate all of my children's learning, and I do it in unique ways for each of my kids. I truly love my life.

Bumping Up Against Other Beliefs

A lot of people are used to being told how to live a mainstream life. Most people follow the herd and never choose to ask themselves about their own truths. When they decide to learn about unschooling, they may think, *Okay, I am choosing to leave mainstream thought, so now I have to learn this whole new way of being with my children.* They search for the *script* of the way to be a "good unschooler." They

63

are quite surprised when they learn that radical unschooling lives are not scripted.

Living how another radical unschooler lives is impossible
because living this way requires living your own truth.

Unschooling is an organic, authentic way of life in which you must blaze your own trail through respecting and honoring your individual children and your own beliefs about the world.

Our unschooled children will naturally bump into other concepts or traditions outside of our own world as a family. We honor and embrace this and are willing to grow and change as a result. As their partners in life, we are willing to explore different religions, diets, activities, cultures and values. We are willing and eager to grow as a family and individually. We learn from our children as much as they learn from us.

Extend Respect to Everyone

Living this life, we choose to extend respect to everyone in our lives, including our own partners, friends and relatives. For a while, my husband was into a show called, *Orange County Choppers*. This is definitely not something that interested me, but because my husband enjoyed the show, I began to embrace it. One day, I thought to myself, I could apply the same philosophy to my husband that we live with the kids.

That night I went online and ordered him a book, *Build Your Own Chopper*. You should have seen how in love he was when I gave it to him; he looked at me and said, "Thank you so much." At that point I knew that I had reached another level of enlightenment. I knew that I needed to embrace everything my husband loved for us to be closer and more connected. Since this understanding, our relationship has become even closer.

The connection that occurs when embracing where others are, instead of where you are at or where you *think* they should be, is a huge shift in learning to connect with others authentically and respectfully. Learning this betters your relationship with people. I love that I can extend everything I have learned in unschooling to the world around me, because it is more than an educational or parenting philosophy. What a huge contribution we can make by starting in our own homes, with our personal values of supporting passions and personal choices of everyone with whom we connect. How rich our lives will become! How much joy we will bring into our lives and the lives of others!

Chapter Six

Parenting Choices

The child is a foreigner who doesn't know the language, isn't familiar with the street plan, is ignorant of the laws and customs of the land. At times he likes to go exploring on his own; when things get rough, he asks for directions and help. What he needs is a guide who will politely answer his questions.

Janusz Korczak

Natural learning is an evolutionary approach to education. Our parenting choices support our children's intrinsic ability to learn what they need to be happy and successful in their own lives. Other parents ask me how I make myself available to four children whose interests constantly shift. What happens when their interests conflict?

In our household, when needs conflict, we share what we want to do in any given day, and we work out a plan to meet everyone's needs. Time can be a factor in our decision making if my son wants to go to the library, but my daughter wants to go to the playground. We talk about the library closing at 4 PM. When I share this with Dakota, she can see the importance and logic of going to the library first, and she is

66

willing to do so. A peaceful solution involved everyone in the decision making process. The children know that everyone's needs are valid and important, rather than me dictating an agenda or a solution. I ask the kids what they think. I am always impressed with options that they bring to the table. We work as a team to find ways to make sure everyone gets to do what they want everyday.

Needs & Behavior

Let's review the obedience model, which purports that something is wrong when a child is not obedient or conforming to authority. So much so, that our culture resorts to drugging a child into obedience. It is stunningly disturbing that a school or parent would change the chemistry of a child's brain to satisfy their own parental needs - the epitome of narcissism. Children are forced through punishments and rewards to act in a manner that eases the parental role. Such coerced behavior meets parents' needs, but rarely takes into account the children's needs. We need to look deeper and realize that we are not here to train our children to be obedient. We are here to raise free-thinking, strong, confident individuals.

As parents living the radical unschooling philosophy, we focus on the needs underlying our kids "behavior." I put behavior in quotes because I feel the word itself is demeaning. I wouldn't say to my husband, *Honey, I didn't like your behavior at the store*. This doesn't feel respectful to me and sounds like terminology used for dog training. For the sake of clarity, I will use the term in the following discussion.

Traditional parenting focuses on a child's behavior. Living the unschooling life infers that we choose not to focus on how *our* child is expressing their needs or their behavior. **I don't judge behavior because I trust that our kids are doing their best through self-expression at any given time.** When parents stop a child's behavior through punishment, they may feel that their job ends at that point. The child's need underlying his or her behavior was not met however. In fact, correcting a behavior rarely meets a child's need. We don't listen to our kids. We just silence them and make them behave.

A critical point to remember and internalize is that a child's unmet need does not go away. Silencing the behavior does nothing for the child and only meets the need of the parent. The child's need is still there, present, not getting met. How overwhelmingly frustrating for a child, or any human for that matter!

Do you know how maddening it is to ask someone for something you really need if you are tired and grumpy, only to have them say, *I don't like the way you asked for that. Sit there for 5 minutes and be nice!* Moreover, they walk away and leave you. Can you feel the frustration build within you? Parents treat children this way every single day, and it warps them internally so much.

Again, the unmet need doesn't go away. Often, the need morphs into another symptom like stuttering or nail biting or something more distressing. Then, we drug kids or bring them to therapy to do away with these troubling behaviors that WE caused! Their need does not go away because you force them to stop expressing it. If only their need was heard in the beginning. If a child could truly have fulfilled her

68

fundamental need to be listened to, this vicious parenting cycle would never have started.

You cannot punish children's needs out of them. Whatever is inside of them that needs to come out will do so, eveen when suppressed. The point is *to notice the need,* and when the need is met, then notice the child's growth: *Wow. She did not scream for her juice that time. She asked me politely. That was awesome.* Just notice and be authentic. Be in the moment and be grateful.

Boredom

Children say, *I'm bored,* and parents' first culturally conditioned responses are like punitive, *You have all those toys, and you are bored? Why don't you go outside? Go find a friend. Find something to do.* Are we punishing children for bringing their needs to our attention? Find that part of your parent-self who will be rebellious against punishment-type parenting. Why not ask simply, *Do you want me to help you find something to do, or would you like to do something with me?*

My husband takes joy in being a rebel to traditional parenting. We will go into a store, and my daughter might ask for something. Joe says, "Well of course you can have that, Ivy" Joe is proud to be kind and respectful to our kids in public. To buck the traditional parenting norm, you have to flip a switch in your brain to respond in new ways. You can recondition your responses and learn to react more joyfully in situations that may have stressed you out before. If your child is bored, you can click a switch in your brain that allows you to get excited when you hear that,

69

suggesting something like, *Cool! An opportunity to do something fun together. What do you want to do? Want to bake a cake?*

I am not saying you won't be tired or frustrated. Your kids can tell when your energy may be down or low. Sharing that you need to do something low key because you are tired is being true to yourself and authentic. Living this life doesn't mean you have to be "on" all the time, creating amazing games and playing until you pass out. Sometimes just going outside can shift your energy level. I like to make fairy houses with the kids in our yard, or lie on a blanket and look at the clouds. This is relaxing for me and they love to do it too.

To renew your own interest and energy, ask yourself: *What do I want to do right now with my child? What am I willing to do right now?* Being present with my kids is very important, and if I am doing something I don't enjoy, my kids know I am not there mentally and get frustrated. **Be honest about your own needs and they will learn to be honest with theirs.**

Unschooling Moment

The concept of living a life in a partnership paradigm takes a while for people to grasp. We were raised to think that control, no matter how subtle, is the way to raise children. Living a radically unschooled life proves that there is another way!

I was in the grocery store the other day in the produce section with the kids. Ivy grabbed a bag and started filling it with brussel sprouts. She was proclaiming her love for this food that many adults have a strong aversion to. There was an older woman watching us in amazement. Ivy squealed with delight and was singing, "I love my brussels! Yeah, yeah yeah!"

I could see that the woman wanted to say something to me, so I said, "Hello." She said, "Wow, you sure trained your kids well!" She was in awe that a child would eat brussel sprouts voluntarily and wondered how I *made* her like them, that somehow it was *my* creation having a child adore brussel sprouts. Some strange form of Jedi mind control? She said, "What's your secret?"

I told her matter-of-factly that I just loved them myself, and my daughter wanted some of that joy. I told her she was never made to eat them and wondered what all my enjoyment was about. The woman looked puzzled at my response, but smiled.

Most people are amazed that through living a truly free life, our kids have many more opportunities and options available to them. When someone is living a life being forced to live someone else's ideals, their future is warped because they lose true choice. Choices made from a power struggle become you vs. them. Long after the choice was made, the power struggle continues.

I believe that so many people hate brussel sprouts today because they were forced, coerced and bribed to eat them as children. Just the sight of a brussel sprout brings people back to that place of having no choice or control over their lives. By nature we so want to "win" that power struggle and are making a huge statement of our own power by not eating certain foods as adults.

Ivy loves brussel sprouts because she has always had the freedom to choose. I love them too, and I never eat them in enjoyment with the *ulterior motive* to get my kids to also. This is something that many coming to this life need to understand. Living life in the present, authentically, is easy once we drop our cultural armor. Most of us were raised with ulterior motives of subtle or overt control, so my perspective isn't coming from a place of a new, tricky way to get our kids to do what we want.

The best gift we can give our kids is to live an authentic life. Communicating respectfully and kindly while shedding the cultural ideas that we must have ulterior motives to "train" our kids can be so freeing and joyful. True, there are ups and downs in life, but no longer are we "in pursuit of happiness." We are living it!

Commitment to Life

A commitment to a radical unschooling life is different. For sure, this is a commitment to living fully with awareness. There is a reason why you came to radical unschooling. Most people come to this life because they want more than they see in the traditional parent-child relationship. They might instinctually feel like they are going against who they are by nature when punishing and living in an authoritarian paradigm with their kids.

People come to this life because they want something different than they lived as a child. Maybe they know deep down that there has to be another way, a better way to live than what they see in the world today. They may see other families living this way and have a new desire to reprioritize and put family, freedom, connection and joy on the list above a school's agenda.

Our culture puts education first and then squeezes family in as an afterthought. This type of unnatural prioritizing infringes on families' freedoms and true purpose. What an unfulfilling and mundane way to live.

This way of life is picking up momentum. More and more parents are opening their eyes and taking power into their own hands to give their family more joy, more freedom and more choices in learning than ever before in history. An awakening is occurring and I am proud to be helping people come to this understanding and way of life.

When prioritizing the tenets of a radical unschooling life at the top of your values list, an education will happen naturally and authentically as a result of living and sharing a full, interesting, passion-driven life together.

Embracing a true shift to a radical unschooling life can be challenging because there are times when I want to sit and do something without interruption. I argue with reality. There is no "without interruption" in my life unless everyone is asleep. I know I have to have realistic expectations. I live in the space of knowing that it is my *choice* to live this life with my children. I know that I have made this commitment to facilitate their learning and it is a big responsibility that I take seriously.

Learning to drop everything to help one of them at any given moment is all part of my role. I know if I get annoyed every time I stop what I am doing to help them, I would be frustrated or mad much of the day. I've learned to *roll with punches* and embrace *what is*. I know I have the choice to help them in either frustration or joy. I choose joy, and everything else follows that.

Because our true needs are met rarely as children, we think, *Now it's our turn to put our needs first... finally!* However, we are the pioneers on the forefront of change! We must release this cultural "me" training and step into the partnership paradigm. Accept and practice the responsibility to learn, right along side our kids. Know what a difference we are making for future generations who will be able to live this life by default because we gave them the gift of being the ones to change the course of parenting history.

The Public Eye

We get asked often about our kids being socially acceptable. Another parent at a conference posed this issue: If you are out in public, and people have no clue that you are unschoolers, and your kids are being loud and crazy, how do Joe and I deal with it?

My response in that situation is that I have established a dynamic with my kids already; a paradigm of trust exists between us. When I offer information about appropriate behavior, my kids appreciate that information. They really do. If I let them know, they trust me on it. They know it is not a power struggle. I am not against them. I am simply giving them information. When I tell my ten-year-old, "It is not okay to be running around in this place", he will say, "Oh, okay." He appreciates and understands. He *wants* to know what is expected wherever we are.

When you feel your kids are "behaving badly" at the mall or in a store, you get creative. You could have them help you find the groceries you need. You could leave. Joe sometimes takes the kids to the gumball machines or to pick out a candy or to the lobster tank to shift the energy before he returns to his shopping with them. In these situations, I remind myself that patience and calmness is all that is needed and anger and frustration will only make things worse. Recognize and honor when your kids need a break and take the time to focus on their needs. Your need to shop is important, yes, but so is theirs to wander the toy or candy aisles slowly, while commenting on all the fun and yummy things that they see. If you are

74

making the choice to take them with you, expecting them to follow behind like little obedient minions is unrealistic. Expect to take time for them to explore, ask questions and pick out some snacks. Rushing is stressful, so if I do not have the time to take them along in partnership, I go shopping by myself.

If you were visiting a foreign country, and you had a guide to share the customs with you, how would you relate to them? If you were told that it wasn't appropriate to show the soles of your feet, you would be grateful that you were given the information! Living this life is that same kind of dynamic. **When you are living a life in partnership, there is no power struggle, hence what others would view as "bad behavior" doesn't happen often because my kid's needs are respected and met.** It's that simple.

You can share with your kids what is acceptable in a peaceful, kind, respectful way, where they appreciate your information. Your approach is all about your energy. I feel it is my responsibility to share information with my children. I think it is a disservice for them not to learn what is acceptable in common situations, because then we would be sending them out into the world without important information. Yes, our kids learn through watching how we are in the world, but discussion is important too. This type of unique parenting dynamic of being our children's guides on their life adventure is a large part of the radical unschooling life.

Most of us were raised in an authoritarian mindset where we had two choices: Obey or be punished. Living this unschooling life enables you to be creative and realize that there are *always* more than two choices. Once on a flight to Florida, Ivy, my three-year-old was talking loudly. A woman got right in my face and said, "You need to shut that little girl up right now! She is being too loud and I cannot stand it!"

Of course, two choices flashed through my head. Obedience to the woman and saying, *I am sorry.* That is *so* not me anymore! I also could have told the woman off, which did flash into my mind, but is also not part of who I am today.

Instead I took a deep breath, and I chose to smile and nod. There was no rule that children on the plane could not talk. The people in front of us turned around and told us that they couldn't hear Ivy at all. I said to the woman, "We will see what we can do," and I winked and smiled. That was it.

I never said anything to my kids. Ivy didn't really notice what happened, and we went on playing. It was important to me that my children saw me react in a peaceful, kind way. Our kids learn from all we do in life in every interaction. Devin and Dakota were watching this and saw how to handle a confrontation respectfully. I didn't get defensive, because I remember my favorite phrase by author Byron Katie: *Defense is the first act of war.*

I become the parent I want to be more and more every day. I have been on the unschooling path for ten years, and I still have back steps sometimes. I need you to know that it is so normal to have those regrettable moments. When you feel guilty about something as a parent don't beat yourself up. I've been there, but now when

I have what I call "back-steps", I know that guilt only attracts more negativity into my life, so I am understanding and kind with myself as much as I am with others.

Chapter Seven

Two Steps Forward, One Step Back

Life is learning, and life rocks!

Dayna Martin

Imagine that your two kids were fighting over a DVD. What would an unschooling parent do? How would you handle that in a perfect, radically unschooled world?

Sometimes we hear the fighting, and it sets off our alarms. Our primitive response is, *Stop it. Stop the noise. Stop the fighting.* From our cultural training, we tend to do the quickest action possible to stop the activity, even if it is not fair for everybody. Finding win/win situations and compromises, on the other hand, takes focus and the time to respond. It is important to understand that our unschooling responses take longer than obedience training. However, the rewards are immeasurable and do not have the negative side effects of traditional parenting.

I might respond this way to children's arguments, *Hey guys, what is going on? Can I help? Can we all work together to figure this out?* Another standard phrase I use is, *Do you guys have any ideas of how everyone could be happy right now?*

You are way ahead in the parenting game if you are the kind of parent you want to be more than half of the time. Realize in the beginning that back steps of falling into traditional parenting mode are common. We find gratitude during these back steps because we are learning what type of parent we don't want to be. Through the back stepping, we can compare what we've learned culturally to the unschooling skills we want to practice. We feel what it is like to be out of alignment with our truth, our authentic parenting. When feeling aligned, we know for certain that we are on the right path.

I remember a time when Dakota hated getting her hair brushed. She is a very sensitive child, and I find ways to make her life easier. On the day of the hair brushing incident, we rushed around to get to a dental appointment. I began brushing her hair, and she got really upset. Despite her distress, I continued to brush it. She cried and told me that she hated me. She said she would never let me brush her hair again, ever.

This whole episode caused us to be late anyway. I feel that I could have handled it so much better. I could have waited for us to arrive there, and then asked her to brush it. She would have been more receptive and calm having not been caught up in my morning rush.

This may sound like a common parenting scenario, but in our home, it is not common. Feeling disconnection, sadness and fear from my daughter enabled me to tap my inner knowing and find a creative solution. There is always a better way than parenting from fear, force or coercion. We must choose to trust rather than be fearful. Trust your feelings if you sense you are imposing upon your children's space. Most likely, you are.

In the end, I was grateful for the hair-brushing experience in order to feel the incredible, contrasting emotions. Learn from such contrasts when you move out of the respectful place. When you can find gratitude for your back steps, rather than marinating in guilt, more goodness and gratitude enter your life. Guilt only attracts more situations to feel guilty about. Always find gratitude in every interaction and celebrate these back steps as personal growth.

Parenting with Authenticity

How you as a parent respond to your child is different for each of us, depending on what feels authentic. You do not have to shift from a mainstream parenting script to the perfect Unschool parent script. There is no script. An unschooling parent's role is to be authentic and do what feels right while balancing respect, kindness and trust for your children.

When intense or negative situations happen, you back step; that is, you have a parenting moment when you are parenting in a way that you do not want. Don't stay stuck in that space. Rather, look at the broader perspective: *you had a wonderful learning experience that makes you a better parent.* Move from regret and guilt to appreciation and joy. Two steps forward, one step back. Can you see the gift in understanding this process of personal growth?

I love to promote authenticity: just being ourselves, which can look different from day to day. One day, you might respond to spilled milk by saying, *Oh my gosh. Let's get a towel and clean this up.* At other times, you might say, *Oops. No big deal.*

The point is you don't have to have a script with a *right* answer all the time. You are real and authentic, expressing natural feelings. Your kids learn how to be in life from watching how you live. You are communicating authentically, without anxiety about *What should I do? What does mainstream culture say I should do? Now it is time for a time-out. Sit in that naughty spot for five minutes. Now apologize to Mama.*

You also do not have to swing to the other side of scripting what you think is the good unschooling response. **Respond with understanding and respect as the default and let the words flow.** A scripted, unnatural rote response ignores your children's needs and puts the focus on you being a good parent. Don't worry, just be in the moment.

Unschooling Moment

Devin has always been very interested in different cultures. Shortly after he began learning about the Mayan people from a great documentary on television, we booked a Cruise to the Caribbean with a stop in Mexico so he could see the Mayan ruins and pyramids. We are all learning some Spanish before the trip in 2010.

Since visiting the different cultures in the Epcot Center at Disney, Devin developed a passion for the Chinese culture. He told me he really wants to go to China. My next mission is to plan a trip there somehow.

Our kids are able to immerse themselves in their interests without someone telling them when to start or stop what they are doing.
They move on to another topic at their own directive, not because someone is hurrying them through. They are able to learn whatever what they want in depth.

Devin will more than likely spend every day for the next week writing and speaking.

Chinese. So far this week we have scoured the internet for images of China. We have watched every video and TV show we could get our hands on about Chinese culture. We went out for Chinese food with our friends the other day too, which was so much fun! The list goes on...

It is 11pm at night right now and when most kids are asleep, my son is still up, exploring his current passion. I'm off to bed, but before climbing the stairs to cuddle between my warm babies, Ivy and Orion, I gave him a hug and kiss and said goodnight. When kids are interested in something, they learn it because they want to and they enjoy it. They can spend as much or as little time as they need on something, which I think is personal and precious.

There's no forcing, no coercion, no grades or measuring of their knowledge. Nothing gets in the way of their dreams and goals. Unschooled kids learn just as much as kids in school but knowledge varies from child to child and is completely catered to them as individuals.

I have no doubt we'll be visiting China someday as a family. Meantime, Devin and I will add something to our family vision board...an image of "The Great Wall of China".

Self Love and Understanding

We radical unschoolers are on the leading edge of new thought. We are on the leading edge of parenting. We are in a new parenting era, shifting consciousness and awareness about what it means to be a family and what our parental role really is. The unschooling journey can be hard because we were parented so differently than how we are parenting now. When we have a moment where our reserves are low or we don't know what else to do, we sometimes reach from our parenting past, recalling what was done to us and how we were treated as children.

Be kind to yourself in these stressful moments and know that you do the best you can with what you know at any given moment. Apply this philosophy to yourself. After all, your children learn to treat themselves as you treat yourself. As you struggle to do it for you, remember that you do it for them.

There comes a moment on the radical unschooling path when you stop moving through the motions of this philosophy. At that moment, you are living the philosophy. You have found your truth.

If you decide to lift children's limits on watching television, but you struggle with inner conflict about trusting your decision, your children will pick up on it. You are not allowing authentically them to be free because you are only going through the motions. Without truly stepping into knowing and believing in radical unschooling, you cannot see or experience what living a life without limits can really be like.

Our kids are so in tune with us, especially those who have been raised in an attachment parenting style. They feel our energy stronger than our words. You may say, *Enjoy as much TV as you want. I trust you.* If you really don't trust them, your kids will know and respond to your inner conflict differently than a parent who truly embraces this philosophy in body, mind and spirit.

Even more important than what you say or do is how you honestly feel and what energy you use to convey your feelings.

Radical unschooling philosophy understands that the connection we have with our kids is beyond physical and we must learn to be true to them and us. Our kids can spot lack of authenticity a mile away. I love this about who they are.

Finding Your Balance

When people first come to this life, they often believe that we are not focused on meeting the parents' needs as in traditional parenting. They feel the pendulum must swing entirely in the other direction to focus solely on meeting the child's needs. This is either/or thinking that was engrained into us growing up in our culture. Unschooling is a beautifully balanced place in the middle of these two extremes.

People tell me that unschooling did not work for them because of their false perception that a parent has to do whatever the child wants all the time, whether they like it or not. They put their own needs on the back burner. They sacrificed all their desires for those of their kids. This is not what unschooling is, and such misperceptions lead people to have negative ideas of what this life is about. Unschooling is not a "you vs. them" paradigm. Unschooling means finding ways to honor everyone's needs at the same time. This is being done by hundreds of thousands of families all over the world as they live this radical unschooling lifestyle.

We are demonstrating how world peace can well be accomplished. We are living a dream that most people can't comprehend, hence the either/or way of misunderstanding this life.

This philosophical shift is part of the educational process for many coming to this life. Another common occurrence on the path after someone learns about unschooling is that the parent knows the negatives of being authoritarian and punitive, but doesn't know what to do to replace traditional parenting practices. They know what they want, but not how to get there. They interpret this life as being totally hands off. In the unschooling community these parents are often given the label of "unparenting."

I've seen anger and frustration from parents on the path to unschooling. They do not interact or offer information to their kids, thinking that this translates to *freedom*. I have learned that this is an important part of the learning curve for such parents. They know what they don't want, and are in the process of learning how to be with their kids. Some parents will never continue on the path of learning their new role, but most will. We can extend the same love and understanding to those who are half way here, and know that they are doing the best they can with what they know at the time, just like all of us.

We can offer them support and mentorship when we notice they are confused about their role as radical unschooling parents. This paradigm shift is huge, a big deal in the course of human history. We are pioneering changes in *everything* we thought we knew about parenting, respect and freedom. Applying this radical philosophy to everyone we meet will catapult the shift in thinking. By truly living what we believe, our children learn that this is a wonderful way to be with others. **Moving from control, judgment and frustration to connection, understanding and kindness is paramount in the lives of both our children and ourselves.**

The Power of "Yes"

My daughter, Dakota, is extremely intense. She does not like hearing no, ever! So I find a way to get to "yes" in some shape or form. I do not mean that I am necessarily dropping everything to do it that moment, but may say: *Oh, that would be fun. I would love to play Candy Land with you. Just let me finish this.* I keep energy with Dakota positive, upbeat and connected. The second she feels any kind of "no" energy, she pushes back, and a power struggle ensues between us.

Yes, power struggles are a common, traditional parenting occurrence, but I refuse to be the wall that stands between Dakota and her wants in life. I let her know that I am her partner. Dakota is a very powerful creator. She wants what she wants, and I honor this about her. I also honor the fact that I can't drop everything every time she wants, but I let her know that "yes" it's going to happen. I focus my dialog on the positive possibility with her. She trusts this, and even helps me finish what I am doing so we can move on to what she wants to do. I have learned the delicate balance of ensuring her that emotional and physical needs are met as well as my own.

Since Dakota was two years old, she screamed if I took too long to bring her something she wanted. For most parents, our old parenting voices haunt us in these intense situations. You may think: *I feel like a slave. My child is pushing me around.* Yet, your other side knows: *She is doing the best she can. I am supposed to help her. I am her partner.* Focus on her needs, not her behavior. Then your mom's voice speaks up, *Do not let her talk to you that way.* In the beginning stages of learning a new way to parent, we often have these contrasting voices visit until we find one that feels best. This is so normal.

It is important for me to follow through with something I have told my kids that I would do. If I say that I will play Candy Land after I finish what I am doing, I make sure that I do. Nothing chips away at the trust more between parent and child as when a parent continually puts a child off and never does what they promised. My kids call me on this if I forget and remind me. I am able to be honest and in integrity with what we live, and I apologize with the same sincerity as I would if I forgot an important lunch date with a friend.

We All Have Fears

I had fears years ago that this parenting approach was not working, because Dakota was so intense. So I would ask myself: *What am I doing wrong? Is this not supposed to make a child be more patient and less intense, and if I treat them kindly, are they not supposed to be instantly kind?* I discovered I was using this kind of parenting early on to control her. I had to realize that my intention behind my actions when she was two and three years old was not in the right place. *I am doing the right things, but my intention is not in the right place. I recognized that it was another form of control . . . I was using peaceful parenting to try and control my child.*

Is that not a weird thing to even think about? But I did not realize at the time I was doing it. Only through the passage of time did I realize how respectful, peaceful parenting worked with her personality. For some kids, you see instantly that kindness begets kindness. For others, you need time. So if anyone has ever thought that this is not working, we have been there too. Believe me! This parenting philosophy is not a new, gentler way to control your child. It is moving from control to connection.

One in four kids are highly intense or sensitive according to some recent statistics. After learning this, I wondered if being more intense or sensitive was just the normal, natural state for my little girl. Following a traditional parenting paradigm, I see that Dakota's spiritual nature would be squelched even though her sensitivity will never go away. She would be drugged and punished, and in turn, those amazing qualities that will be her driving force to chase her dreams in life would be robbed from her.

Her intensity is going to help her as an adult. She will always get what she goes after. She will not take no for an answer when going for the career she wants. She will be passionate and focused. **Everything that our culture views as negative**

in a child is what we celebrate in an adult. So why are we drugging this out of kids today? To make the lives of the adults who interact with these kids easier.

I am so proud that I can see who my daughter truly is and know, from the broader perspective, that her intensity is a gift to celebrate.

Proof Is Not In The Results

Traditional parenting is a results-based paradigm. When unschooling however, we watch our children learn something new and share the excitement. The great thing about living this life is being part of those first discoveries. What an honor! External motivation isn't necessary, nor are incentives or rewards. Children learn because they want to, not because they want to please anyone else.

Maybe you have a fear of the future when you see kids' negativity. Maybe another day, you don't feel up to the task of facilitating their learning. Parenting authentically allows us to speak up: *I can see now from how she is acting that this is more important than I thought.* **The freedom unschooling offers the parent is the permission to not have to be right, not have to be consistent, and not have to listen to all of the cultural voices that you think you have to.**

You may even have moments of being *real* when you yell at your child, and then you apologize authentically and say: *I am sorry I yelled, honey. I am so hungry, and I get really irritable when I don't eat when I should.* My kids now will say: *Mom, you need to eat something.* They know that about me, even my four-year-old, Ivy. She knows that if I am grumpy that it isn't about her, or her fault. She

89

knows that I have needs that have to be met to feel good again. By meeting and valuing my kids' needs and focusing on them rather than their behavior, they have learned this about other people too! I can see it everyday. They are caring, understanding and loving, learning from the way we are with them.

Apologies are good and real and human. There is nothing you cannot make up for. Children will learn that too. My child will yell, and I have heard her apologize to her sister. You do not have to be perfect. We strive to be the best parents we can be. Learning a new way to parent our children takes time. We are not awful parents because we have moments when we act in the way that we were parented. If we can be the parent we want to be more than half the time, we are ahead of the game! We are perfect, because we are being authentic and we have the good intentions to support their freedom, respect, peace and joy.

Chapter Eight

Respectful Partnerships

Be who you are and say what you feel because

those who mind don't matter and those who matter don't mind.

Dr Seuss

Learning Curves Allowed

One aspect of unschooling that I address often is how to help someone's partner understand this life if one parent arrives at this life before the other. When one partner is learning about this new parenting philosophy they may feel so enlightened that they begin to scold their partners for being punitive or authoritarian. It can be challenging applying this same philosophy of respect, kindness and trust to our partners in the same way we do with our children.

It is important that I walk the walk, not only with my kids, but with my husband too. Focusing on Joe's needs, which underly *his* actions was hard for me in the beginning of our journey. If he yelled at the kids, I would get angry and tell him what he was doing "wrong." This escalated into negative reactions from both of us and spiraled us downward as a couple. I have learned over time to focus on Joe's needs as much as everyone else's. I know that he is doing the best he can with what he knows how to do in any given moment.

He rarely yells or takes an authoritarian approach to parenting now, but if he does, I don't feel that he needs punishment or scolding any more than the kids do for anything. I respect and open my heart to understanding that he has to walk his own path. Our lives have never been better since I have applied this philosophy to him as well as our children, and everyone else in my life.

I can ask, *What are you frustrated about honey? How can I help?* In the way that we help our children, we can also help our partners get what they want in life. **Becoming aware of the importance of our partner's needs as much as our kid's needs and our own is so vital to harmony in the family.**

If our partner is new to the unschooling path, I extend the same respect to him to learn in his own way and time, as I do with our children. I understand that the only way someone learns is from internal motivation, not from another person telling you what to learn or how to learn.

Unschooling encourages us to trust our partners as we practice what we preach. When we are learning a new philosophy, a way of life, like radical unschooling or peaceful parenting, one of us often becomes the research junkie, reading message boards, books and new information.

It is a double standard to have that peaceful, respectful philosophy with our kids, but not with our partners, or others in our lives. This is a whole life philosophy. I suggest you give yourself time to talk, read, and share about radical unschooling together.

It has taken a long time for me to shift from control with my husband when I saw him doing something that I would not do. If he yelled at the kids because he was frustrated, I used say: *Stop yelling. You are hurting them. You can at least be kind, because kindness begets kindness.* I went into lecture mode of teaching him how to parent wonderfully, like I felt I was. However, my actions were counterproductive because my kids were learning conflict from me. I was not promoting peaceful parenting because distrust and conflict was the backdrop of our parenting relationship.

The best thing that I have learned to do is to release control and let my partner be the parent he needs to be. Each parent has a unique learning curve.

This is how we grow as parents, through experience. Growing is like climbing up a ladder. On this unschooling path, we just keep going. This path includes parents helping parents, not listening to experts.

How else can our children learn except by seeing how we interact? Merge into partnership. Partners don't want to hear, *Do not yell. Why are you doing that? You are going to hurt them!* Instead, find out *how* your partner is in need. What is his or her fear? What emotion underlies the need to yell? How can you help them in the present situation?

Also, I think fathers are supposed to parent differently than mothers. Embracing that natural aspect of life was huge for me. Mothers and fathers, by nature, are different in how they go about parenting. Joe does not have to be just like me and do what I do. What a revelation to discover that he didn't have to parent exactly like me for us to live in harmony together as a family.

Unschooling Moment

One unschooling mother shared this story: *My husband has had a hard time trusting himself, so he tries to parent like me. He does not know what to do, so he follows my style, which does not really work for him. So, I feel this huge burden to always do it right and always be perfect. That is an issue for us.*

This was my response: The majority of society does not parent in an unschooling way, so a parent has to feel confident to follow her intuition, because it is the natural way of doing things. Some dads are looking for a more formal guide or education in how parenting is supposed to work. The more you have the radical unschooling philosophy imbedded in you, then you naturally respond to your children and partner in a peaceful way.

An unschooling dad once explained his viewpoint to me: "I think the women have the instinctual side because they are with their babies. I think for the dad, it's too easy to lapse into the same patterns we were raised with, because a dad is used to being told for twenty, thirty, or forty years: "Yes, no, don't do that or do what I say.

"Then suddenly your wife says, 'No. We are not doing it that way.' Even if dads get used to a new way and like it, we still find it hard to sand those ruts down, because we are so entrenched in dad's and granddad's way."

Some dads feel a loss of power when they don't know what to do. In their frustration, they may say to their partners, *Well, you do it then, because you obviously are the one who does it right*. A dad may not know how to find his instinctual way of parenting because of his own upbringing and culture.

This brings a question to my mind. *Is instinct the way you were parented? Is that part of instinct? Or is instinct totally primitive?* I can see in my partner the instinctual part of him that wants to be the authority. He wants to be obeyed. He wants the children to listen to him. It's his turn to be heard after being parented for so long in an authoritarian paradigm.

The whole need-for-obedience thing is huge for most fathers. I can see that it is easy for me to not expect obedience, because I have lived the partnership paradigm from the beginning and practicing attachment parenting. But for him, I feel bad sometimes, because it looks like parenting is not what he thought it would be.

Joe's Perspective

When asked by moms how best to deal with a partner who wanted to lay down the law vs. moms who wanted to support their children, Joe responded in this way: "I remember Dayna's gentle ways of telling me that I should hold off. It is hard; no matter what she would say, I would feel defensive, because that is what we men generally do. That is why we are still fighting wars today, because we get defensive."

Joe suggests that you can say gently to your partners, *Do you think we can try this just for a minute?* How can you ask them in a gentle, kinder way? If they still don't get the concept I would pre-pave the way by saying, *I would like to try something the next time so-and-so is flushing your shaver down the toilet. Can we try something else without you being defensive or angry?*

Or try this statement, *I am not telling you we should do this, and I do not want you to get defensive.* It is a cycle of defensiveness. Could you say, *The next time so-and-so is pouring the cereal on the floor, can I try it my way, just for once.* Hey, after twelve times, he is going to see that your way is a valid option.

Striving for win/win situations and compromise is the key. I think an intact marriage or intact relationship is the priority for our family, because it is the basis of our entire family in general. In the greater, broader perspective, we honor that and make it a main priority.

De-schooling Buffers

We have always unschooled and lived this natural approach to parenting. If you are someone who is starting fresh with a fourteen-year-old who has been schooled or traditionally raised, or for those of you who are new to unschooling, you may experience a certain de-schooling buffer, the de-lifestyle-change buffer that you will have to go through.

When you start unschooling with young kids, your way of life becomes natural. It is almost easier for us who have always lived this way. It is just life. There is no difference between what it used to be and what it is. Yet, if you are changing from one traditional landscape to a new one, you have to paint a new picture. The terrain changes significantly, and mutual respect for needs is a top priority and much brainwashing must be undone.

Unschooling Moment

I think a lot of us mothers had fear before we started the unschooling journey and learned that we cannot do it on our own. I am certainly not perfect, and I have had days where I thought I had completely fallen off the wagon. Now when my partner comes home, he can respond. He says: *All right. Do you really think that was the right response?*

So, saying to your partner who is not home all day, who is coming along on this path behind you, *Maybe, I am not doing it right and I need to talk about this.* So if you model that to him and say: *I do not really know. I need help. Let's work as a team to figure out the best way to react to certain situations.* We have a common goal.

Work Out A Game Plan

Work out your partnership game plan for parenting, even down to the signals and the words you will use. Remember you can trip other people's energy switches. Know what makes your partner defensive and try never to go there. Respect them in this way.

In our household, Joe will be out in the shop working, and I will have been with all four kids for six hours. On some days, I can feel my patience dipping, and I am becoming the parent that I do not want to be. I will go out to him, and we will be silly and I will say: *I need renewed patience to step in for a minute.* So we will high-five each other behind our backs as if changing teams and say: *You're in! Good luck!*

Next, Joe will be the kids for a while. I pre-paved the way, setting it up so that his ability to be patient comes into play. I could go into his shop and have said: *I am going nuts. These kids are driving me crazy today. You need to go in and take care of them, please.* Then Joe would think: *I am going to help you. I am going to fix them. I am going to go in there and rescue you.*

This isn't what I want in the moment. I may just want someone to take over while I take some time to recharge my batteries.

How I present my words, demeanor and intention to Joe invites his rescue or high-five responses. If I go to him and say: *King of Patience is your cup full? Can you go do it for me, Babe?* He will go to the kids with that patient, heart presence. That has been huge for me to learn through trial and error.

Humans learn through doing. When I see Joe parenting in a way that I might not agree with at the time, I think, he needs to do that. That is his journey. It is the process he needs to go through to feel what that experience brings up. So that viewpoint has allowed me to release a lot, too. It has allowed me to release the need for control.

Mutual Respect

Parenting partnerships are authentic and compassionate. We are here to empower our children, each other and ourselves. If you are on the outside looking in, you can say that it works because it appears that the kids are compliant. Once I really understood that kindness begets kindness, it blew my mind. Peaceful partnering and parenting are as simple as that...to be kind and respectful to others will help them learn that it is a great way to be in life.

Our kids are mirrors of who we are and what we do. When you really understand this, everything changes in your interactions. You let go of being punitive and authoritarian and become kind, patient, understanding, loving and joyful. These qualities make people feel good. Isn't feeling good and being happy what life is all about?

Radical unschooling is changing the way we view parenting. Not only that, but the way we view our relationships with others. I love this Maya Angelou saying, "You did then what you knew how to do. When you knew better, you did better." I know that we are all doing the best we can with what we know. I hope that this book will broaden what you know as truth and bring you to a new level of awareness about relationships with your children and your partner.

Radical unschooling requires that we surrender to the present and give up thinking that things should be different. That is when we suffer. If we think circumstances should be different than what they are, you suffer. Realize that things should be exactly as they are in your life right now.

Your kids are perfect in all that they are doing and living. Living a happy life now means living a happy life in a week and a month and a year from now. It means looking forward to a happy childhood and lifetime. This is the secret that we have all been searching for. Embrace it.

Chapter Nine

Living in Awareness

All that you are is a result of what you have thought.

Buddha

I want to share some of my personal philosophy which is integral to my radical unschooling philosophy. I have noticed that my personal growth as an unschooling mom is an ever-evolving and continuous process. I was never really spiritual before having kids and coming to this life. Radical unschooling is such a powerful process of living in the now that it touches every area of my life. It is so much more than just a parenting or educational philosophy.

Everyday, I focus on staying positive and trusting not only in my children, but also in my universe. Moreover, I take the responsibility for my thoughts and this has become my priority. I never want to fall back into the fears I felt as a first time mom. I learned that fear begets fear, just as trust begets trust. My choice is clear!

Do you ever feel that when you have a bad day, your energy ripples through the household, affecting everyone in various ways? I know that if Joe or one of my kids is in a bad mood, we all feel it and are affected by it, if only subtly. One thing is definite - we have to develop the inner resources which allow us to be aware of our thoughts and feelings and how they affect our family members. Most people think this requires some kind of vigilance. For me, however, vigilance is tiring. Awareness is a matter of relaxing with my children, trusting the universe, and staying in a place of gratitude and positive moods.

This ripple effect, as in respect begets respect, in radical unschooling works through the power of your focus or awareness. **Whatever you focus on is what you expect and receive.** A good example of the ripple effect is my son Devin's story.

He went kayaking with my in-laws, who have three kayaks. Devin loved it so much. He came home and said: "Mom, I so want a kayak. I really want to get one." Many parents would have responded with a doubting energy: *Ah, when you are older,* or *You are going to have to save your money.* And the child may not have thought about it any further, following the energy of the parent.

Living in awareness and connection with Devin, I said, "All you have to do is *feel* what it will be like to own it. Your universe will line everything up for you to get one. Thoughts become things. Picture what it would feel like to be getting your kayak. Feel that excitement and trust that one will be coming to you. Picture yourself plying down the river and be excited about it." Two days later, I was driving by a yard sale and there was a kayak for twenty-five dollars.

I drove home and said: "Devin, there was a kayak for twenty-five dollars that had a tiny little hole that Daddy could patch with a kit." Devin was so excited that he wanted to pay for it with his own money. We offered to pay for it for him, but he wanted to do it himself. We drove together back to the yard sale and tied it to the roof of our car and brought it home. Devin manifested his kayak, and I am thrilled that he experienced the positive success of his focus and trust that he can have anything he wants in life, just by trusting and understanding his own power.

The trust you have in your children's ability to learn, the trust that you have for the way you are living your lives, is extended to the universe through knowing that you are going to get what you want in life, material or non-material. Here is an example. Imagine that you are telling yourself repeatedly, *We do not have enough; we do not have enough money.* In this scenario, you will never have enough money because this is the order you are continuously placing with the universe. The same is true in living this life and knowing how powerful we are. Whatever you think about and focus on is like an order placed to the universe. Whether you see it as good or bad, the universe always delivers.

If you want money, you have to learn to love money. Love it. Be grateful for what you do have and hold your awareness and focus there. Nothing new can come into your life unless you are grateful for what you already have.

Staying in a positive, joyful mindset as much as you can will draw more experiences into your life that gives you those feelings. Like attracts like when it comes to your feelings. Just as Devin breathed excitement as he kayaked across the lake, you also can marinate in the gratitude for what you have. You can affirm for yourself that you are happy that you have enough money to live this rich, abundant, radically unschooled life. That is how you bring more in, by loving and being grateful for what you already have.

You focus on what it is that you need or desire, and then you turn it over to the universe. Act as if it has already been resolved or that you have already received what you want. Then be open should you receive something different than what you asked for. Often times the universe will give you something better than what you desire.

The principles in play are awareness and attraction. For example, when you are first pregnant, you suddenly notice all of the pregnant people around you. You never saw them before because pregnancy was not in your awareness, even though pregnant women have always been around you.

You buy a new car. Suddenly, you see the same car everywhere. They were always there, but you are only aware of them now because of where your focus is. The principle of focusing on your thoughts is the same idea. You focus on what you want, and you will see it and find it. Everything you want is there already, but if you do not think you deserve, you are not going to see it.

I would have been blind to a kayak had Devin not focused on his desire. Because I live a radical unschooling life and trust my son and the universe, I was open to seeing the possibility also. Trust and possibility are in my awareness. Always!

Vision Boards

Vision boards come in handy for being able to visually focus on what you want in life. A vision board can be a cork board or a poster board, for which you cut pictures or words from magazines, graphic images of desires or dreams from your computer, or draw and color. What you love in life and what you desire to manifest go on your vision board. Always in sight means always in your focus, and always growing in your awareness. Post your vision board in a prominent location!

I made a vision board three years ago, and most of the things on it have come into my life. Good health for our family is on my vision board, and we rarely get sick. I put a cruise ship on my vision board because I always wanted to go on a cruise. I put an RV on there too. I posted a microphone, because I love to speak about unschooling. You get the idea? Since the time I created my vision board, we bought an RV, are going on one cruise and I am traveling the globe speaking about my passions. I believe that seeing my desires and thinking about them everyday aided me greatly in getting what I want out of my life.

In our unschooling lives together, we can use our focus and positive energy to create our utopia for the next generation of children.

Life Happens

At conferences, I have heard all of the negative things that happen to people, and they tell me they find it hard to focus on positive attitudes or gratitude because of their life circumstances.

- "My seventeen-year-old daughter doesn't believe in being positive; won't our desires for different lives clash?"

- "My husband died, so I know bad things happen. How can I trust the universe?"

- "My son doesn't trust me, and I don't trust him. How can we focus on creating a more positive atmosphere together?"

Each time I present at a conference, I could say, *Your only job is to feel good,* and then I could leave. This is the basic message, said in a million different ways. **If you feel good, good feelings bring good things into your life.** That is the reality! You create your reality by what you focus your attention on. You do not ever have to convince anyone of your reality. No one else has to believe it to make it true for you. Your only job - joy of being - is to feel good.

I am not saying you must make everything perfect all the time, because we are human, and we think negative thoughts. We all agree that life happens, and from the broader perspective, everything happens for a reason. The power of focus can seem magical when events are synchronous, like the way in which Devin's kayak appeared. However, it is not magical or mystical; it is awareness of the energy you put into your world with your thoughts and feelings.

106

More and more people are taking the responsibility for their lives by learning that their thoughts become reality. Our children have this awareness and it is wonderful for them to understand that they are not corks floating on the ocean. They are very powerful creators, and they can have anything that they want in their own lives.

Chapter Ten

Unscooling Realities

Life doesn't happen to us; it happens from us.
Charles E. Swindoll

Positive thoughts are uplifting. Optimism gives us hope. However, true to radical unschooling, being authentic does not include pretending, being a martyr, or giving every last ounce of energy to our children before we pass out. Recall from previous chapters that communication, caring, compromise, prioritizing and shifting awareness are all tools that help us be real, upbeat, and happy as parents on this path.

Get Authentic

We do have meltdowns sometimes, and we discuss those normal human moments of fatigue, doubt, and frustration. We apologize when we act in ways that we wish we didn't. I think my kids, who are raised with secure feelings of attachment, are very in tune with my husband and I on many levels. Many of us come from an attachment parenting background before we step into the unschooling journey, and we know our kids can read our energy better than they ever comprehend our words.

For example, have you ever noticed someone walk into a room and instantly you felt whether you liked or disliked the people or person there? You just knew. This is energy, or vibes, so to speak, that you are feeling. This is an instinctual feeling, not a random reaction that came to you. Our kids feel this type of energy from us so strongly that even if they don't know how to articulate it, they certainly know what we are feeling instinctually.

Let's say your child wants to play with you, and you feel that you should play with her as a good unschooling parent, thinking: *I guess I should do this because it is what I am supposed to do.* Yet, your kids sense that you do not want to be doing what you are doing, and that is conflicting for them. They feel you not being present with them. I think that those moments of being authentic and honest about your feelings are better than being conflicted and going through the motions. *Honey, I'm not really in the mood for this game right now. Is there anything else that we could do together?*

One thing that I have learned while living this life is that a positive, joyful "no" is twenty times better than a negative-feeling "yes" with anyone in our life, not just our kids. I want my children to know that they can be authentic and clear in their desires. I want them to understand that saying yes to something if they really don't want to do it rarely results in a good time for anyone involved.

Upbeat All Day?

I think a new person learning about radical unschooling philosophy might feel that us unschooling moms dance around singing about rainbows and butterflies all day long. We don't! **Just because happiness is something that is very important to me, doesn't mean that it is my only emotion all the time.** Also, I hear at conferences that people think that they have to shift attitudes by going from dragging to soaring in 6 seconds. Hey, the good news is that neither is true.

We don't zoom from fear to optimism and joy. In fact, that is an unnatural way to shift moods. There is an emotional scale that can make the task of shifting moods easier, and we can be more realistic with our children. For example, imagine yourself climbing an emotional ladder, where each rung is an emotion that feels a tiny bit better than the last. Which emotion is a bit better than fear? Insecurity? What's a bit better than insecurity? Jealousy perhaps? Move through the gradually improving feelings of hatred, revenge, anger, discouragement, blame, worry, doubt, disappointment, frustration, boredom, to contentment, hope, optimism, enthusiasm, happiness, passion and joy, empowerment.

Fearful or depressing feelings throw a parent, and often the whole family, out of balance. When you feel negative emotion or desire to move out of fear or depression, let go of the idea that you have to dramatically change your mood. Moving quickly from fear to joy might be too far a stretch.

Don't give up because you are feeling down one day. Remember the ripple effects of emotions and thoughts. Don't think, *I cannot trust, so forget it. I am staying in this downer place.* You don't need to stay there, and don't need to leap to another feeling that feels too far away. Work up gradually to a more positive feeling emotion or mood. When you focus your energy on something more positive, just one degree at a time, you will find yourself more in control of your emotions and more equipped to take responsibility for your life.

Raising Our Vibes

Another way to shift your mood or energy to a more positive note is called raising your vibration. Because we know we are made up of pure energy and our thoughts and emotions are also energy, you can raise your vibration by remembering joyful moments with your family. Doesn't remembering the first time your child called you mama or mommy make you smile? Do you remember the way it felt when your family members were all piled up on the couch together, happy and content? These are the memories that you can pull into your awareness to aid you as you are shifting moods and feeling better.

To raise my vibration, I do things that bring me joy and make me feel good. Sometimes the easier choice is to stay in that negative mindset. I've heard this called *lazy thinking* because you are not taking responsibility to pull yourself out of your dark mood. You just choose to stay there and complain about it physically and emotionally.

It has taken me years to learn how to choose peace of mind and to send pleasant ripples of good feeling throughout my household. I tell myself: *I have to do this. No one is going to do this for me. If I want to raise my vibration and be in a better place, I need to take the time to...* This process is called shifting or pivoting your thoughts. I pivot my mindset by going online and reading an inspirational story, visiting a message board that I enjoy, listening to loud, heavy metal music, or walking outside.

What makes you happy? What can you do to raise your vibration when you are down? Once you can raise your vibration, everything follows on that same vibrational scale. If you are feeling tired or irritated, it is amazing how everything can appear so glum and awful. You see through an entirely different set of lenses than if you were in a place of joy.

When you establish the habit of raising your vibration, you'll find it easier to stay happier longer. A conference participant once asked me, "How do you fit that in...like, it would be nice to be able to stop and shift and get positive, but you have four kids yelling, and dinner needs to be made, and it is getting late...?" I believe that my trust in my self-management is the truer answer than discussing more strategies. I am confident that I will get everything done, and I always do. My key choosing not to worry about getting it done or the timing of how it will get done. Worrying is a future-based mindset, and I have learned to live more in the present. This is one way to live in joy rather than fear.

112

As far as keeping the house clean, I feel grateful for our space, feel true gratitude for each task I perform in caring for a home. As I clean up scraps of paper from the floor, I remember the craft project we did together. I focus on how grateful I am to be healthy and active. I find the gratitude for every task in my life. In doing so, it is easy for me to keep my house clean. I pick up toys and think, *I am so grateful that my kids are healthy and that I have this beautiful home and that they have these toys.* My focus and my thoughts are on gratitude, and I establish a habit by focusing on it. The more I do this, the more this type of thinking becomes my default way of thinking and being.

Here is another example. I had no unschoolers in my geographic area a few years ago. There was nobody around, and boy did I beat that drum: *There are no unschoolers. I am the only one. Oh, it is such a lonely place to be. Why aren't there more people like me?* Not a good place to be as all of my focus went into a black hole of poor me! This went on for years. I know now that I was continuously sending that order out to the universe that there were no unschoolers in our area.

The universe continuously gave me what I was focusing on, over and over again until I changed my focus and thoughts. I later did change my thinking and began to feel gratitude for the online unschooling friends that I had. I also told myself things like, *I can picture myself hanging out with others on this path. I can feel myself spending time with free, connecting families. It is going to happen.* Guess what happened next?

I got an email from a woman who said, "I am moving from Colorado to your town. I know about you. We are a radical unschooling family." Two weeks later, another person contacted us who was from the next town over and moved to our town. Now, we have an unschooling community, a group that gets together. This shift in thinking and experience inspired me to start a non-profit organization called *Unschooling United* which offers parent-to-parent support through monthly meetings and phone help. I know from experience that if you build it, they will come!

Chapter Eleven

Advocacy

Never doubt that a small group of thoughtful, committed citizens can change the world. Indeed, it is the only thing that ever has.

Margaret Mead

Be Your Own Advocate

Joe and I had an incredible experience as the featured guests on the *Dr. Phil Show* and advocating for radical unschooling. We knew going public as advocates of the unschooling way of life might bring some controversy. The public's first response to anything new is usually opposition. However, after the discussion on the show, I felt that Dr. Phil opened his mind a little about the topic.

Not everybody wants to be an advocate and face opposition, but I am willing to do that because I trust the process of change and know that first comes opposition, then possibility, then acceptance and then a shift to common practice. It is the natural flow of acceptance of any new idea or way of life.

I can smile in the face of opposition because I am taking a step in the right direction on behalf of unschooling. Also, many people do not understand the philosophy of unschooling, so they may judge this way of life on unfounded perceptions.

Learning that there is another way of life, in contrast to the traditional systems of both education and parenting rocks the foundation and very core of many people. It can be shocking to learn that parenting with punishments is unnecessary, after all, most people feel that they are essential in raising a child. Learning about this life can lead to fervent questioning of so much of what people think is necessary to get from point A to point B.

When people learn that a more joyful, connected and respectful way to be with their children is possible, their unfolding new reality can be intimidating. The freedom of this new life scares them. When someone judges this life without fully understanding it, I embrace their reaction and open my heart. I know that through learning about this life confusion and frustration often follow. Healing from the past is usually necessary before stepping into this awareness.

Advocacy comes in a variety of forms. For example, being kind to your child in public is a simple step in advocacy. By proudly being an example for other parents to follow, you are modeling this new parenting paradigm. At conferences, I ask other unschooling parents, *What type of advocacy are you drawn to if you are not an advocate right now and you want to be?* I hear some of these comments:

- "I used to cringe when I shared with others that I am an unschooler, knowing that their reaction may be negative. Now, I am at a place where I am happy to

116

share this life. No one has to agree with me. Not only that, but I also see other parents being kinder to their kids when I am around. This is how I know I am an advocate."

- "Sometimes I do not share my beliefs with other people, because I just don't want to get into it. You do not mind opposition; however, I have a hard time with it. I would like to understand how to be in that place of confidence."

People laugh when I tell them that I had an incredible fear of public speaking before becoming a parent. In school, I was terrified of being in front of a class. I was the shyest person you would ever meet. I would throw up the night before an oral report in school. Even in college, speaking in front of others was extremely difficult for me.

I have come a long way, and it is rewarding to help people and speak about what I believe in. I have learned that when someone is forced to speak in public, as in school, it can be debilitating. However, if a person has a message they believe in passionately, their words flow easily.

Being a public advocate for unschooling, I have had to learn to have thick skin and be secure within myself. I know now that how I represent this movement isn't about me, but the truth that needs to be told. My calling is to help shift awareness about the rights and respect that children deserve. I believe so strongly in the life we are leading that I am willing to put myself out there. I know that opposition is just a step toward the process of acceptance.

Confidence and security go hand-in-hand with the unschooling life. You understand and live so much more than any words can convey. How peaceful, kind and lovingly you carry yourself and how you interact with your kids speaks louder than any words.

On The Dr. Phil Show, speaking our truth was very important to us. Joe and I discussed the show beforehand and we agreed that we only needed to be ourselves, answer honestly and be peaceful and respectful no matter what anybody said to us. This way of being is the basis of the life we choose to live with our children.

One time on our way to a conference, a woman asked us where we were headed. I explained that we were going to an unschooling conference. She asked what that was. I explained that with ninety-nine percent of homeschooling families the parent buys a curriculum and does school-at-home at the kitchen table. We do not approach learning in that way. We have a lot of different learning resources. We strive to live a happy life, chasing our passions all day. This is one way in which I might explain our method of homeschooling to others. I always smile and share in a non-confrontational way.

Legality

A major point discussed at conferences is the legality of homeschooling. It is important to me that I share that we are promoting a legal form of educating our children, albeit outside the box. It is on the fringe of the homeschooling movement, but *it is a method of homeschooling, nonetheless.*

It is important for you to do your research in your own state to learn the requirements. Some states do not require that you report anything, where others do. A great way to find out about your state's homeschooling laws is to do an online search for "Unschooling in New Hampshire", for example. Joining local online discussion groups for unschoolers in your area is another great way to connect and ask questions about your state's requirements.

If you are fearful about becoming an advocate, it is best to follow your feelings. Follow what feels right with regard to how you want to advocate: a blog, writing articles, being kind to your child in public, hanging out with a friend for tea while explaining a little bit more about how you choose to live your life with your family. Your options are limited only by your imagination. What I do know is your advocacy must bring you joy. If you feel passionate about what you are sharing with the world, your joy ripples through others. We are all advocates when choosing to live this amazing life. **We are making history and raising consciousness simply by living in freedom and respect with our children.**

Unschooling Moment

I had no idea that we would be advocates.

It just happened so gradually and naturally.

The same thing might happen to you when your authenticity sparks other people's

inspirations. You cannot force advocacy because it is born from your bliss.

It happens authentically and naturally. It is not something you can force and can

sa *I am going to be a public advocate now.* You follow your bliss.

It is the same with birth or breastfeeding advocacy.

When I get a breastfeeding call, I am electric. I love helping a mother and

reassuring her that her child is doing exactly what she should be.

I love sharing that same enthusiasm about unschooling. For me, advocacy is the

love of helping people have a more peaceful life with their kids, because I see the

joy and relief in a parent when I share: *You do not have to make them do that.*

They may say: *Really? I can be happy? We can connect and just do what we want?*

I love being part of this light bulb moment with other parents.

Commonalities with Others

I am understanding of people's viewpoints and respectful of their desire to know or
not know about the radical unschooling philosophy. I do not judge others who
choose a traditional parenting paradigm. In fact many of my friends live very
different lives than we do. So how do we make a friendship work, while making
such different choices for our families?

I think it is culturally common to focus on differences we have with others. We
isolate ourselves this way. This cultural default way of being makes us feel alone,

even in a group of people. We live in a time of one-upmanship and competition. We compare our kids' milestones with others. We focus on how our friends are parenting differently and are determined to feel our way is best. As a culture, we seem to thrive on making ourselves feel better by putting down other people's choices.

For me, moving from the traditionally cultural way of interacting with others has taken me years, but has been worth every moment because it is all part of my self-growth. I can see that my children have learned to focus on the good in others. They honor and respect diversity and live with a mindset of acceptance because we now live this way.

Defining this goal as a parent has encouraged me to find another way to *be* with others in my life. One way I do this is by focusing on what I have in common with other people. If my neighbor loves gardening and I also enjoy it, then I connect through that commonality. Why focus on how we parent differently when we have so much in common in other ways? We might enjoy the same television show or hobby. It is a choice how we choose to relate to others. We can choose to live on this planet isolated, feeling terribly different in our choices, or we can find ways to connect with others through our commonalities.

We talk about our commonalities, not our differences. I do not focus on what we do not have in common. My goal with everyone I meet is connecting with them.

When you face opposition or negativity about your choice to live radical unschooling life, instead of taking it personally and letting that affect your life, just smile and know that all is well. The only important point is knowing that you are on the right course for *you*. Know that it is never about you personally, but the ideas you represent.

Advocacy is promoting a better quality of life for other families. Even if someone isn't interested in full-blown radical unschooling, your connection with them will allow them to be kinder and gentler with their own children. For example, your conversation with someone may mean that a parent doesn't punish her child with time-outs anymore. When a friend sees how you interact kindly and lovingly with your own children, it will enable them to have the courage to think outside the traditional parenting box and give their own children more freedom and respect just by simply being around you. Little ripples of change make big differences.

Conclusion

We are bettering the world by living the truth contained in this book. We are effecting the course of human history. Perhaps through radical unschooling we are helping to shift toward peace on earth. I'd like to believe so. I am so grateful for this opportunity to help in the awakening of parents everywhere.

The World needs our Children!

Join the Revolution!

~In Joy & Gratitude, Dayna

AUTHOR

Dayna Martin is a passionate, radical unschooling advocate who enjoys traveling the world speaking about her unique and joyful family life and inspiring others on their path.

Dr. Phil invited Dayna and Joe Martin to be his featured guests on the **Dr. Phil Show** in 2007 where they introduced 50 million global viewers to radical unschooling and respectful, peaceful parenting. Dayna takes part in various radio and television interviews regularly. She is an inspiring speaker and writer, who has been published in several magazines and books worldwide.

The Martin family love being together all day, everyday chasing their passions and living the life of their dreams.

www.Dayna-Martin.com